Mastering SEO: A Comprehensive Guide to On-page, Off-page, and Technical SEO

4

Module 1: Introduction to SEO

Lesson 1: What is SEO? – An Overview

Definition of SEO

SEO stands for **Search Engine Optimization**. Imagine SEO like this: the internet is a huge library, and websites are the books. When someone types a question into Google (or another search engine like Bing), they're looking for the right "book" with the best answer.

SEO is a way to make a website look interesting and useful to search engines so they want to "show it" to people searching.

In simpler words, SEO helps websites be found more easily on the internet. If you own a website or a blog and want people to visit it, SEO makes that possible.

When you type something like "best pizza near me" into Google, you'll see a list of websites about pizza places nearby. The websites that pop up at the top have great SEO because search engines think they're the best match for your search.

Evolution of SEO: Past, Present, and Future

SEO has changed a lot since it began in the 1990s, and it keeps changing as technology improves.

The Past

In the past, SEO was simple. People would put a lot of words, even if they repeated, on their website pages. If you had a website about toys, you might just repeat "toys" all over the page.

Search engines would think, "Wow, this page must be all about toys!" So they'd show it to anyone searching for toys.

But this wasn't the best because the pages didn't always have the best information. They just had lots of words.

The Present

Today, SEO is much smarter. Search engines now look for websites with the best answers. They want sites that are helpful, interesting, and easy to read.

Just repeating words doesn't work anymore. Instead, websites that have clear, helpful information and show that they really know the topic are the ones that appear at the top.

Search engines also look at other things, like how fast the website is and if people find it easy to use on their phones.

The Future

In the future, SEO might get even smarter. As technology improves, search engines could understand more about how people feel when reading a website or know exactly what people want without needing many words.

Some experts even think we could talk to search engines like we're talking to a friend.

Overall, SEO's future is about making sure people get exactly what they need easily.

Why SEO is Crucial for Online Visibility

Online visibility means how easy it is for people to find you on the internet. SEO helps a website pop up higher in search engine results, so more people can find it.

Think of it like this: imagine a toy store hiding in a big city with no signs pointing to it. Hardly anyone would know about it. But if the store had big, bright signs, people would know it's there and might come visit. SEO is like those bright signs for a website.

When websites are easily found, they can attract more visitors. This is super important for businesses, schools, hospitals, and anyone who wants to be noticed on the internet.

Here are a few reasons why SEO is important:

1. **More People Find You:** Good SEO means more people can find your website. For a business, this can mean more customers.
2. **Building Trust:** When a website shows up at the top, people believe it's reliable. That's why companies want their websites to be on top.
3. **Free Traffic:** SEO helps websites get visits without paying for ads. If a website ranks high, people can find it naturally, so there's no need to pay for every visitor.

A Fun Fact About SEO:
Over 90% of people only look at the first page of

Google results. This means if your website is on the second page or lower, most people won't see it. SEO helps get your site to that important first page.

Joke 😄

- "Why did the SEO expert go broke? Because he couldn't get any clicks in real life!"

Quick Recap

To sum it all up:

- **SEO** is a way to make a website more noticeable on the internet.
- SEO started simple but is now all about helping people find the best answers online.
- In the future, SEO will keep getting smarter, making it easier for search engines to show us what we're looking for.
- SEO is super important for making sure websites can be found online, building trust, and getting visitors for free.

Joke 😄

- "How many SEO experts does it take to change a lightbulb? Just one, but they'll need to optimize the light switch, add keywords, and wait a few months for it to rank!"

Pro Tip 💡

- *Start simple with SEO.* If you're new, focus on creating great content and learning basic SEO terms. As your knowledge grows, so will your site's traffic!

Lesson 2: Importance of SEO in Digital Marketing

Welcome to Lesson 2! Today, we'll explore why SEO is so important in digital marketing and how it can help businesses grow.

We'll also compare SEO with PPC (another way to get noticed online) and learn how SEO fits into a digital marketing plan.

Why is SEO Important in Digital Marketing?

Imagine you have a lemonade stand. You want people to know about it so they can buy your lemonade, right?

Now, picture that the internet is a huge neighborhood with thousands of lemonade stands. How will people find yours? This is where **SEO** comes in.

What is SEO?

SEO, or **Search Engine Optimization**, is like putting a big, bright sign on your lemonade stand saying, "Best Lemonade Here!"

It helps search engines like Google notice your website. When you have good SEO, Google puts your website at the top of the search results. And when people see your website first, they're more likely to click on it.

How SEO Helps Businesses Grow

Just like with the lemonade stand, businesses use SEO to help people find them online. When more people visit their website, they have a better chance of getting more customers and making more sales.

Let's look at some real-world numbers to understand how big SEO is:

- **93% of online activities start with a search engine** – When people look for information online, they often start with Google, Bing, or another search engine. SEO helps businesses get noticed during these searches.
- **Over 60% of people click on the first 3 search results** – That means if a business is one of the top 3 results, it has a much higher chance of people visiting its website.
- **SEO can increase website traffic by over 300%** – With strong SEO, businesses can get three times more visitors than before. More visitors mean more chances to make sales.

SEO is like a friendly guide helping people find their way to your website.

Benefits of SEO for Business Growth

Now, let's break down why SEO is so helpful for business growth.

1. Brings More Visitors (Traffic)

Imagine you have the best lemonade, but no one knows about it. That would be sad, right? SEO helps spread the word.

When people type keywords like "best lemonade near me," your stand will appear at the top if you have strong SEO. This way, more people come to try your lemonade.

2. Builds Trust and Credibility

When people see a website at the top of Google, they trust it more. Just like if everyone says your lemonade is the best, more people will trust and buy from you. SEO helps your website become one of the most trusted sources in your business area.

3. Brings Long-Term Results

SEO isn't a one-time effort. When you work on your SEO, it keeps helping your website for a long time. Even after you stop updating, SEO still brings visitors to your site. It's like planting a tree; it grows and provides shade for years.

4. Saves Money

SEO doesn't cost as much as other ways of advertising. Once you're at the top, you get visitors for free, without needing to spend more money. It's like word of mouth – people keep coming because they heard you're good!

Joke 😄

- "SEO is like working out – you don't always see results immediately, but when you do, everyone notices!"

SEO vs. PPC: Pros and Cons

Now, let's talk about another way to get noticed online: **PPC** or **Pay-Per-Click**.

What is PPC?

PPC is like putting up a billboard for your lemonade stand. You pay for every person who sees or clicks on your ad. For example, you might pay $1 each time someone clicks on an online ad to check out your lemonade stand.

Pros and Cons of SEO and PPC

Method	Pros	Cons
SEO	- Free visitors once you rank high	- Takes time to get top results
	- Builds trust and credibility	- Needs regular updates
	- Long-term benefit	- Hard to predict when you'll see results
PPC	- Instant results	- Costs money each time someone clicks
	- Easy to control who sees the ad	- Once you stop paying, traffic stops

So, both SEO and PPC have benefits and downsides. A mix of both can work well, but SEO is especially good for long-term success.

The Role of SEO in a Digital Marketing Strategy

A digital marketing strategy is like a recipe for success, and SEO is an important ingredient.

SEO as the Base

SEO is the foundation of any good digital marketing plan. Think of it like building a house – SEO is the strong foundation that supports everything else. When you have a strong SEO, other things, like ads and social media, work even better.

How SEO Works with Other Digital Marketing Parts

1. **Social Media** – SEO helps people find a business's social media page too. When a website ranks high, its social media often shows up, which means more followers and likes.

2. **Content Marketing** – Good SEO means writing helpful and interesting content. When people find and enjoy this content, they're more likely to share it, which helps SEO even more. It's like making a fun lemonade recipe that everyone wants to try and share.

3. **Email Marketing** – If visitors come to a website through SEO, they might sign up for emails. This means the business can keep in touch with them. And the more visitors they get, the more email subscribers they have.

4. **PPC Ads** – When you have strong SEO, your PPC ads can be more effective. For example, people who see your PPC ad are more likely to

trust it if your website also shows up in regular
search results.

Joke 😊

- "Why did the website need therapy? It had too
  much 'site anxiety' from low search rankings!"

Pro Tip 💡

- *Remember the "3 C's" of SEO: Content,
  Consistency, and Creativity.* Engaging content,
  a steady posting schedule, and creative ways
  to connect with users will boost your online
  presence.

Lesson 3: Understanding Search Engines and How They Work

1. What Are Search Engines?

Think of a search engine like a super-smart librarian.
Just like a librarian knows where every book is in the
library, search engines like Google and Bing know

where to find all the web pages on the internet. They help us find answers to questions by searching through millions of websites.

Joke 😄

"Trying to understand search engines is like trying to solve a Rubik's cube – every time you think you've got it, there's another twist!"

2. How Do Search Engines Find Websites?

Imagine there are millions of new websites created every day. Search engines need to know when a new website is made or when an old one is updated. They do this by "crawling" the internet.

- **Crawling:** This is when a search engine sends out "spiders" or "bots." Bots are like tiny robots that visit every page on the internet. They hop from link to link, just like a frog hops on lily pads, to discover new pages.

- **Indexing:** After finding a page, search engines save a copy of it in something called an "index." An index is like a giant book of all the websites and what's inside each page. So, if someone searches for "fun facts about space," the search engine knows where to look because it has everything saved.

Joke 😄

- "Why did the search engine break up with the website? It said, 'It's not you, it's your *bounce rate*.'"

3. How Do Search Engines Rank Websites?

When you search for something, the search engine doesn't show you all the websites it knows about. It shows you the most helpful pages at the top. But how does it know which page is best?

- **Algorithms:** This is the search engine's secret recipe, like a special formula. The recipe looks at lots of different things to decide if a page is useful. Some ingredients in this recipe include:

- ○ **Keywords:** If you search for "cute cat pictures," search engines look for pages that use those words.
- ○ **Page Quality:** If a lot of people like a page or share it, the search engine thinks it's good and ranks it higher.
- ○ **User Experience:** A website should be easy to read and work well on computers and phones.

4. What are Ranking Factors?

Ranking factors are the things search engines look at when deciding which websites to show first. Here are a few simple ones:

- **Relevant Words:** If the page has words that match what you're searching for, it's a good sign.
- **Website Speed:** Pages that load faster get ranked higher because no one likes to wait.
- **Security:** Secure sites with "https" in the address are trusted more.

- **Links from Other Websites:** If other websites link to a page, it's like giving that page a thumbs-up.

5. Differences Among Major Search Engines (Google, Bing, etc.)

- **Google:** Google is the most popular search engine. It looks for the most accurate results and has a very detailed "recipe" or algorithm that changes often. It's always trying to be super helpful by showing exactly what people want.

- **Bing:** Bing is another big search engine. Bing often looks at things a bit differently from Google and may show slightly different results. It's known for focusing a lot on images and videos, so it's great if you're looking for something visual.

- **Yahoo!:** Yahoo! used to be super popular. Today, it works with Bing, so when you search on Yahoo!, you get results from Bing.

- **DuckDuckGo:** This search engine cares a lot about privacy. It doesn't track you, so it's good if you want to keep your searches private.

Pro Tip 💡

- *Focus on user experience!* Search engines love sites that load quickly, are easy to navigate, and offer valuable information. Keep these in mind to rank higher.

Lesson 4: Key SEO Concepts: Keywords, SERPs, and Ranking Factors

What Are Keywords and SERPs?

Keywords

Think of keywords as the main words or phrases people type into Google when they want to find something. Imagine you're looking for a new toy.

You might type "best toys for kids" or "fun toys for 8-year-olds." Those phrases are **keywords** because they help search engines understand what you're looking for.

Website owners also use keywords so their sites show up when people search. If a website uses the right keywords, it's easier for people to find it!

SERPs (Search Engine Results Pages)

SERP is just a fancy way of saying the page that shows up after you hit "search" on Google. This page displays lots of options for you to click on.

The top results are usually the best matches for your keywords. If a website has good SEO (which we'll talk about soon), it can appear on the first page of these results, making it more likely that people will visit that website.

Impact on SEO

When websites use the right keywords and have good

SEO, they are more likely to show up high on SERPs. Being at the top of a search results page is like being the front display in a store; more people will notice it and click on it.

Joke 😄

- "Why did the SEO keyword cross the road? To get to page 1 of Google!"

SEO Ranking Factors

There are three main parts to SEO: **On-page, Off-page, and Technical SEO**.

1. On-Page SEO

This means everything on the actual page of a website that helps it rank higher on Google. Imagine you're creating a website about the coolest toys. Here's what makes up On-Page SEO:

- **Title Tag**: The title that appears in the search results. It should be catchy and contain keywords like "coolest toys for kids."

- **Headings**: These are like titles for different sections of your page and help organize content.

- **Content**: The actual words, pictures, and videos on your site. Good content has keywords, is easy to understand, and provides useful information.

- **Image Alt Text**: This is a description of an image on your site, which helps search engines understand what the picture shows. It's like telling Google, "This is a picture of a fun toy."

2. Off-Page SEO

Off-Page SEO is all about what happens away from your site that helps it rank better. Imagine people at school talking about how cool your website is—that's similar to Off-Page SEO. Here are some important parts:

- **Backlinks**: These are links to your website from other websites. If other good websites link to yours, it's like a vote saying, "Hey, this site has cool information!"

- **Social Media Shares**: When people share your website on social media, it makes more people visit, which can help your site look popular to search engines.

3. Technical SEO

This is the behind-the-scenes work on a website. Think of it like making sure all the pieces of a toy work together smoothly. Some important parts are:

- **Mobile-Friendliness**: The site should look good on a phone and a computer.

- **Page Speed**: How fast the site loads. Nobody wants to wait forever for a page to load.

- **Security (HTTPS)**: This makes the website safe for people to visit.

Core SEO Metrics

SEO metrics are like scorecards that show how well a website is doing. Let's look at three important metrics:

1. **Click-Through Rate (CTR)**

   CTR measures how many people saw a link to your site in search results and clicked on it. If 100 people saw the link and 10 clicked, the CTR would be 10%.

   Why it matters: A high CTR means people find your website interesting enough to click on, which is a good sign for Google.

2. **Bounce Rate**

   This is the percentage of people who visit your site but leave quickly without looking around. If 100 people visit and 70 leave right away, your bounce rate is 70%.

Why it matters: A high bounce rate can mean people didn't find what they were looking for on your site. Lowering the bounce rate is usually better for SEO.

3. **Average Session Duration**

This measures how long people stay on your site. Longer sessions mean people are interested in what's on your page.

Why it matters: When visitors stay longer, it shows search engines that the content is useful, which can help boost your SEO.

Joke 😊

"How do you know if your SEO is working? When you start feeling like a celebrity because everyone is searching for you!"

Recap

- **Keywords** help websites be found by people searching for something specific.

- **SERPs** are search result pages, and ranking higher on them helps sites get more visitors.
- **On-Page, Off-Page, and Technical SEO** all work together to improve a website's ranking.
- **SEO metrics like CTR, bounce rate, and session duration** are like scores that show how well a site is doing.

By using the right keywords, paying attention to On-page, Off-page, and Technical SEO, and keeping an eye on metrics, websites can attract more visitors and provide helpful information.

Pro Tip 💡

- *Pick keywords wisely.* Go for long-tail keywords that match specific user intent. They may have lower search volumes, but they often convert better because they're more relevant.

Module 2: Keyword Research and Strategy

Lesson 1: What Are Keywords and Why They Matter

What Are Keywords?

Imagine keywords like treasure maps! When people want to find information, buy something, or learn something online, they type words or phrases into a search engine like Google or Bing.

These words or phrases are called "keywords." They are like clues that tell the search engine what people are looking for, so it can show the right results.

Think of it this way: if you type "best ice cream flavors" into Google, "best ice cream flavors" is the keyword. It helps Google understand that you're interested in ice cream options, and Google will show you websites with information about ice cream flavors.

Why Do Keywords Matter?

Keywords matter because they help people find the information they need. They are the link between what people are searching for and what websites offer.

For businesses and websites, using the right keywords is like sending out a signal to say, "Hey! I have what you're looking for!" Without keywords, websites would be like treasure chests hidden without any map to find them.

Here's a fun example: Let's say you have a website that sells pet toys. If you use keywords like "pet toys," "fun toys for dogs," or "safe cat toys," people looking for those exact items can find your website more easily.

Without those keywords, people might not find your website when they need pet toys.

Types of Keywords

There are three main types of keywords, and each one has its own special job. Think of them as different types of treasure maps:

Navigational Keywords

Navigational keywords are like a "find the way" map. People use these keywords when they want to go to a specific website or place online.

For example, if someone types "YouTube" or "Facebook login" in the search box, they're using navigational keywords. They already know where they want to go; they just need a little help getting there. Imagine you have a map that tells you how to get to your friend's house. Navigational keywords work the same way—they guide people to a specific place.

Informational Keywords

Informational keywords are like the "learn something new" map. People use these keywords when they want to find information or answers to questions.

If someone types "how to bake cookies" or "what is the biggest planet," they are using informational keywords.

They're looking to learn, read, or understand something.

Think of informational keywords as the questions you ask when you're curious. Just like you might ask your teacher, "How does a plant grow?" people use informational keywords to ask search engines things they want to know.

Transactional Keywords

Transactional keywords are like the "I'm ready to buy" map. People use these when they are ready to make a purchase or take some action, like signing up for something.

Examples of transactional keywords include "buy a laptop," "order pizza online," or "sign up for a gym." These keywords show the search engine that the person is close to making a decision and is looking for something specific to buy or sign up for.

It's like you saved up your allowance, and you're ready to buy that new toy you wanted. Transactional keywords help websites know when someone is ready to take that final step!

Why Using the Right Keywords is Important for Websites

When websites use the right keywords, they can reach the right audience. Imagine if you were looking for "bicycle repair tips" but all you found were websites selling bicycles.

That wouldn't help you, would it? Websites need to use keywords that match what people are looking for, so they don't confuse their visitors.

Here's a cool fact: Every month, over **8.5 billion searches** happen on Google! That's a lot of people searching for answers, products, or places. Websites that understand the right keywords to use can help people find exactly what they're looking for.

How Do Keywords Work in SEO?

In SEO (Search Engine Optimization), keywords are like secret codes. When a website uses the right keywords, it becomes easier for people to find.

SEO helps search engines like Google understand what a website is about, and keywords are a huge part of that process.

Let's say you want to make your pet toy website popular on Google. Here's how keywords can help:

- **Researching Keywords** – First, you look for keywords that people are using when they search for pet toys. You might find keywords like "buy dog toys," "safe toys for puppies," or "funny cat toys."

- **Using Keywords** – Next, you add these keywords to the text on your website. You can use them in places like the title of your page, in descriptions, and even in picture captions. This helps Google see that your website is all about pet toys!

- **Getting More Visitors** – When people type one of your keywords into Google, Google will see that your website has those keywords and might show it in the search results. More people can then click on your website and maybe even buy some pet toys!

How Websites Choose the Best Keywords

Choosing the right keywords takes some thought. Here are some steps that websites follow to find the best ones:

- **Think Like a Searcher**: They imagine what people might type if they were looking for what their website offers.

- **Use Keyword Tools**: Websites use tools like Google Keyword Planner, which gives them a list of keywords and shows how many people search for each one.

- **Check Competitors**: They also see what keywords similar websites are using.

- **Choose the Right Mix**: Websites mix keywords from all three types (navigational, informational, transactional) to make sure they attract all kinds of visitors.

Fun Fact: Keywords in Everyday Life

Did you know you use keywords every day without even realizing it? When you ask your friends questions or search for videos, those words are your keywords! And just like on the internet, choosing the right words helps you get the answers you need.

Key Takeaways

- **Keywords are words or phrases people use to search for information online.**
- **There are three main types of keywords:**
    - **Navigational** (to find a specific website),
    - **Informational** (to learn something new), and
    - **Transactional** (to make a purchase or take action).
- **Using the right keywords helps websites reach the people looking for what they offer.**

And that's why keywords are so powerful—they connect people and information, like a real-life treasure map!

Lesson 2: Types of Keywords: Short-Tail vs. Long-Tail

Short-Tail Keywords

Short-tail keywords are simple, short phrases usually made up of just one or two words. They're like quick hints about what someone is looking for. Since these keywords are short, many people might use the same ones, so they're very popular. Here's a fun example to understand:

Example: Imagine you want to learn about "chocolate." If you just type "chocolate" into the search bar, you'll get tons of different results – recipes, types of chocolate, where to buy chocolate, and more! This one word is broad, and it could mean many different things, so it's considered a **short-tail keyword**.

- **Data on Short-Tail Keywords:** Studies show that short-tail keywords make up around **30%** of all searches online. This is because they cover big, general topics that lots of people search for.

Quick Facts:

- **Length:** 1-2 words
- **Popularity:** Very high (many people use them)
- **Example Searches:** "Shoes," "Weather," "Movies"
- **Challenge:** It's hard to know what someone wants exactly because the word is too general.

Long-Tail Keywords

Now let's talk about **long-tail keywords**. They're a bit longer, with three or more words, and they help us get more specific about what we're searching for.

These keywords give us a better idea of what the person really wants.

Example: Instead of just searching for "chocolate," you might search for "how to make chocolate cookies." Now, you'll probably get recipes for making cookies, which is what you really wanted! By using **long-tail keywords**, you get more exact results.

- **Data on Long-Tail Keywords:** Long-tail keywords make up about **70%** of all searches online. Because they're more detailed, fewer people search for the exact same thing, which makes them less competitive and easier to use.

Quick Facts:

- **Length:** 3 or more words
- **Popularity:** Lower (fewer people use them, but they're very helpful)
- **Example Searches:** "Best running shoes for kids," "Rainy weather activities for toddlers," "New animated movie trailers"
- **Benefit:** Long-tail keywords show specific intent, meaning you know exactly what the person wants to find.

Differences Between Short-Tail and Long-Tail Keywords

Aspect	Short-Tail Keywords	Long-Tail Keywords

Length	1-2 words	3 or more words
Popularity	High (lots of people search)	Lower (fewer people search)
Competition	Very high (many websites use)	Lower (fewer websites target them)
Search Intent	General	Specific
Example	"Toys"	"Best educational toys for 3-year-olds"

Why Long-Tail Keywords Are Important

So, why should we care about long-tail keywords? Because they can help us find exactly what we're looking for more easily! Let's look at some cool advantages of long-tail keywords:

1. **Targeting Intent**
   Intent means what someone really wants. When someone types in a long-tail keyword like "best chocolate for baking," they're probably planning to bake something and want the right

type of chocolate. Long-tail keywords help us understand people's **intent** better.

- **Example:** Someone searching "bookstores with fantasy novels" wants a specific type of book, while "books" is too general.

2. **Less Competition**
Since fewer people search for long-tail keywords, fewer websites try to rank for them. This means if you're a small business or website, you have a better chance of showing up at the top of search results!

- **Data Fact:** Websites using long-tail keywords can appear on the **first page** of search results more easily than with short-tail keywords, because there's less competition.

3. **Better Conversion**
Conversion means getting someone to take an action, like buying a product, signing up, or

clicking a link. When people find exactly what they want with long-tail keywords, they're more likely to take action.

- Example: A person searching "buy organic honey near me" is likely ready to buy honey, while someone who just searches "honey" might just be curious about it.

Example of a Long-Tail Keyword's Impact

Let's say a toy store is selling educational toys. If they use the keyword "toys," they'll be up against a lot of big toy companies, and their website may be hard to find. But if they use "best educational toys for 3-year-olds," they'll get fewer searches, but they'll reach exactly the right parents who want to buy for their kids.

Conclusion

In this lesson, we learned that:

- **Short-tail keywords** are short and popular but very general.

- **Long-tail keywords** are longer, less popular, and more specific.
- Using long-tail keywords can help people find exactly what they're looking for, face less competition, and are more likely to lead to action, like a purchase or signup.

So next time you search, remember the magic of long-tail keywords. They might be long, but they're super helpful in finding just what you need!

Lesson 3: Using Keyword Research Tools

Goal: Learn about popular keyword tools like Google Keyword Planner, Ahrefs, and SEMrush, and how they help us analyze competitors in SEO.

Introduction to Keyword Research Tools

Imagine you're setting up a lemonade stand. To make it successful, you'd probably check where other kids are selling lemonade, what they're charging, and how many cups they're selling.

Keyword research tools work similarly for websites! They help us find out which "lemonade" or keywords are popular, how other websites use them, and ways to make our stand (website) the best on the block.

Here's how three popular tools can help us understand keywords:

1. **Google Keyword Planner**
2. **Ahrefs**
3. **SEMrush**

Let's explore each one, with fun examples and data to help us understand!

Google Keyword Planner

What Is It?

Google Keyword Planner is a free tool from Google. It helps us find keywords that people are searching for on Google, like "best toy store" or "how to bake cookies."

How It Works

Let's say you have a website about fun science experiments for kids. Google Keyword Planner can help you find out which science experiment keywords people are searching for. For example, it can show you:

- **Keyword:** "Easy science experiments for kids"
- **Monthly Searches:** 10,000 (that's how many people search this each month)
- **Competition Level:** Low, Medium, or High (tells you if other websites are also using it)

Example

Imagine we typed "science experiments" into Google Keyword Planner. We might see results like:

Keyword	Monthly Searches	Competition

"Fun science experiments"	5,000	Medium
"Simple science projects"	3,200	Low
"Home science activities"	2,000	High

With this data, you might choose "Simple science projects" because it has enough searches and less competition, making it easier to rank higher.

Ahrefs

What Is It?

Ahrefs is a paid tool with a lot of information on keywords, including how websites rank for specific words and links that help them rank better.

How It Works

Ahrefs helps with something called **competitive analysis**. That means we can look at other websites that are already doing well and see what keywords they use. For example, if you have a website about pets, you can see which keywords top pet sites use.

Example

Let's say you type "dog care" into Ahrefs to see what keywords successful pet websites use. You might find:

Keyword	Traffic (Visits)	Competition Level
"Dog grooming tips"	15,000	Medium
"How to care for a puppy"	12,000	High
"Best dog food brands"	20,000	Medium

Ahrefs also shows you **backlinks**, which are links from other sites that make a site more popular. If a site has many backlinks for "Best dog food brands," you'll know this keyword is valuable.

Tip

By finding out which keywords work for other websites, you can use similar ones for your website and try to attract more visitors.

SEMrush

What Is It?

SEMrush is another paid tool with lots of data. It gives information on keywords, competitors, and trends.

How It Works

SEMrush offers something called a **Keyword Difficulty Score** to show how tough it is to rank for a certain keyword. The higher the number, the harder it is to rank.

Example

Let's say you have a cooking blog and want to rank for "easy dinner recipes." When you search this in SEMrush, you might see:

Keyword	Difficulty Score (0-100%)	Monthly Searches
"Quick dinner ideas"	40%	25,000
"Healthy dinner recipes"	55%	18,000
"Dinner recipes for kids"	30%	10,000

If you're just starting, a lower Difficulty Score, like "Dinner recipes for kids," might be better because it's easier to rank for.

Trend Analysis

SEMrush can also show if a keyword is trending, which means if more people are searching for it recently. This helps you know which keywords are getting popular, like "holiday cookie recipes" closer to the holidays.

How to Use These Tools Together for Competitive Analysis

When you put all these tools together, it's like being a detective for keywords! Here's how:

1. **Start with Google Keyword Planner:** Find keywords with good search numbers.
   - For example, if you're creating a blog about adventure stories, start with keywords like "best adventure books" and check search volumes.
2. **Check Competitors with Ahrefs:** Look at popular websites in the adventure book space.
   - If a top website uses keywords like "adventure books for teens," you might use that too!
3. **Analyze Difficulty with SEMrush:** See how tough it is to rank for each keyword.
   - If "Best adventure books" has a high score, you can try something similar, like "Popular adventure books for kids" with a lower score.

Quick Tips

1. **Choose Keywords with Enough Searches:**
   You want keywords that people are actually looking for, but not too many other sites are using.
2. **Check Your Competitors:** See what popular sites are doing, and try similar keywords.
3. **Look for Trends:** Use trending keywords to keep your website fresh and interesting!

Using these tools may seem like a lot at first, but with practice, you'll find the best keywords to bring more people to your website. Good luck, SEO explorer!

Lesson 4: Mapping Keywords to User Intent

Introduction to User Intent

User intent is the purpose behind someone's search. When people search online, they're looking for specific information or action. For example:

- **Informational Intent**: When someone wants to learn something, like "How to bake a cake."
- **Transactional Intent**: When someone wants to buy or do something, like "buy chocolate cake online."

Knowing these intentions helps us create content that truly answers what people want. Let's dive deeper into these types!

Understanding Informational Intent

Informational Intent means someone wants to find information or learn something. They're usually not ready to buy but want helpful answers. For example, "What is SEO?" is an informational keyword.

Example:

1. Keyword: "What is SEO?"
    - Intent: The user just wants to understand SEO, not buy anything.
    - Content Idea: Write an article or guide explaining what SEO is in simple words.
2. Keyword: "Benefits of brushing teeth daily"

- Intent: The user wants to learn why brushing is important.
- Content Idea: Create a blog post with tips on brushing and its benefits.

Understanding Transactional Intent

Transactional Intent means someone is ready to act, like making a purchase, booking, or signing up. They're more likely looking for specific services or products. Keywords often include action words like "buy," "purchase," or "sign up."

Example:

1. Keyword: "Buy SEO tools"
   - Intent: The user is looking to buy software or tools for SEO.
   - Content Idea: A product page that lists SEO tools, prices, and features to help the user make a purchase.
2. Keyword: "Sign up for dentist appointment"
   - Intent: The user wants to make a dentist appointment online.

- Content Idea: A landing page where they can choose a dentist and schedule an appointment easily.

Practical Steps to Map Content to User Intent

Step #1: Identify the Keyword's Intent

- Look at the words in the keyword. Ask, "Is the user trying to learn, or are they ready to buy or do something?"
- Example: For "best online drawing courses," we can tell the person wants to find and possibly purchase a course.

Step #2: Choose the Right Content Type

- If the keyword is **informational**, make content like guides, articles, or "how-tos."
- If it's **transactional**, create product pages, booking forms, or landing pages.

Examples:

- Informational Keyword: "How to draw better" – A step-by-step guide with drawing tips.
- Transactional Keyword: "Enroll in drawing course" – A signup form for drawing classes.

Step #3: Write to Match User Needs

- Imagine what questions the user has and answer them. Make content clear and helpful.
- For a keyword like "why is recycling important," break down facts in easy steps and use pictures or data.

Example:

- Keyword: "why is recycling important"
- Write content like: "Recycling saves the Earth! Did you know recycling 1 can of soda can save enough energy to power a TV for 3 hours?"

Step #4: Optimize for Keywords Naturally

- o Place the keyword in the title, introduction, and subheadings naturally. Make sure the content still reads smoothly.

Example:

For "best pizza in town," your article can include "If you're looking for the best pizza in town, we've listed top spots!"

Making Content Intent-Focused

Here's a table to match keywords to content types for different intents:

Keyword	Intent	Content Type
"How to plant roses"	Informational	Step-by-step guide
"Best SEO software for beginners"	Informational	Comparison article

"Buy SEO software"	Transactional	Product page with prices
"Schedule a dentist appointment"	Transactional	Booking page

Using Data to Guide Your Content

Understanding common searches helps you design content that answers those questions best. Here's an example of how data can guide content:

- **Example**: If you find that 1,000 people a month search for "how to brush teeth correctly," you know there's strong informational intent. Create a "how-to" video or article with illustrations, steps, and fun facts.

Quick Recap

- **Informational Intent**: User wants to learn. Content should educate or inform.

- **Transactional Intent**: User is ready to act or buy. Content should guide them toward a purchase or action.

Matching content to what users really need helps them find answers faster and builds trust. Keep your audience's intent at the center, and your content will succeed!

Lesson 5: Building a Keyword Strategy

Creating a solid keyword strategy is like choosing the right tools for different tasks in a big project. For SEO, each type of content, from blog posts to product pages, needs a tailored keyword approach to reach the right people at the right time.

Section 1: Creating a Keyword Strategy for Different Content Types

Blog Posts (Informational Content)

Purpose: Blog posts answer questions, provide tips, and teach readers something valuable.

Keyword Strategy: Focus on keywords that people might search when they need answers. These are usually longer phrases called "long-tail keywords."

Example: If your website is about pet care, a blog post could use a keyword like "how to keep my cat healthy in winter." This is a long-tail keyword because it's a specific question someone might ask in a search engine.

Data: Around 50% of searches are long-tail keywords, and they usually have less competition, meaning it's easier for your page to appear at the top of search results.

Product Pages (Transactional Content)

Purpose: Product pages are for people who are ready to buy or learn more about a specific product.

Keyword Strategy: Use short-tail keywords with clear intent, like "buy hiking boots." These are usually direct and related to products or services.

Example: If you sell hiking boots, a keyword like "best hiking boots for kids" targets people looking to purchase and might help attract buyers to your page.

Data: Studies show that using transactional keywords can improve click-through rates (CTR) by about 30% because people searching for these terms are more likely to click on relevant links.

Landing Pages (Sales Content)

Purpose: Landing pages are focused on driving action, like signing up for a newsletter or downloading a guide.

Keyword Strategy: Include keywords with an action, such as "sign up for free newsletter on pet health."

Example: If you're promoting a free guide about pet health, your landing page might use a keyword like "free guide to pet health," which attracts users interested in getting valuable information.

Data: Websites with clear calls-to-action on landing pages see up to 55% more engagement. Keywords that match these actions help capture attention.

Section 2: Aligning Keywords with Business Goals and Customer Journey

1. **Understanding the Customer Journey Stages**
   - **Awareness:** When customers are just learning about their problem. Use keywords that are more general and provide helpful information.
   - **Consideration:** Customers know what they need and are exploring options. Use keywords that compare or suggest specific options.
   - **Decision:** Customers are ready to buy or take action. Use clear, action-oriented keywords.

2. **Example:** Let's use the example of a website selling gardening tools.
    - **Awareness:** "Why do plants need fertilizer?" helps people who are just learning.
    - **Consideration:** "Best fertilizers for tomato plants" helps them compare.
    - **Decision:** "Buy organic tomato fertilizer" targets people ready to purchase.

3. **Matching Keywords with Business Goals**
    - **Increasing Traffic:** Use informational keywords that answer questions or provide knowledge. This helps bring more visitors to your website.
    - **Increasing Leads:** Use keywords with phrases like "guide," "tips," or "learn more" to attract users interested in more details.
    - **Boosting Sales:** Use strong transactional keywords like "buy," "top-rated," or "best" to target users close to making a purchase.

4. **Example:** If your goal is to get more people to sign up for a cooking newsletter, you might use a keyword like "healthy meal tips" on a landing page to attract people interested in learning about food.

5. **Using Data to Refine Keywords**
   - **Keyword Search Volume:** How often is a keyword searched each month? Keywords with higher search volumes are popular but may have more competition.
   - **Keyword Difficulty:** Some keywords are harder to rank for than others, especially short-tail keywords that a lot of websites want to rank for. Choose a mix of keywords with both high and low difficulty.

6. **Example:** If the keyword "healthy dinner ideas" has a high difficulty, but "easy healthy dinners

for kids" has a lower difficulty, the second option might be a better choice if you're targeting parents.

Section 3: Building a Simple Keyword Strategy

1. **Step #1: Define Your Main Goal**
   - Ask yourself, "What do I want visitors to do on my website?" Your goal might be to increase sales, boost email signups, or improve engagement with your content.

2. **Step #2: List Potential Keywords**
   - Based on your goal, think about what your audience might search for. If your goal is to sell more pet supplies, you might list keywords like "pet food," "buy dog toys," or "safe cat litter."

3. **Step #3: Organize by Content Type and Customer Journey Stage**
   - Place each keyword under the type of content and the stage of the customer journey where it would be most useful.

4. **Step #4: Test and Adjust**
   - After using these keywords, check your website's data to see how well they're working. If a keyword isn't helping, try a new one!

Module 3: On-Page SEO

Lesson 1: Content Creation and Optimization

1. What is SEO-Friendly Content?

SEO-friendly content is like writing a story that search engines like Google enjoy and want to share. Imagine Google as a librarian with billions of books.

SEO-friendly content is like having a book that's easy to find on the library shelf. It should be clear, useful, and have the right "keywords" so that people can find it quickly.

Example:
Let's say we're writing a blog about "dogs." If we use words like "dog training," "fun dog facts," or "how to take care of a dog," we help Google know our story is about dogs. People searching for those terms are more likely to see our blog.

2. Guidelines for Writing SEO-Friendly Content

a) Start with a Good Title
The title is the first thing people see, so make it interesting and clear. Try to include a keyword in the title. This helps search engines understand what the page is about.

Example:
Instead of "Things to Know," a better title is, "Top 10 Fun Facts About Dogs."

b) Use Headings to Organize Content
Headings, like **H1** and **H2** tags, are like chapter titles in a book. They help break down information, making it easier for readers and search engines to understand.

Example:
If you're writing about dogs, you could have these headings:

- H1: **How to Care for a Dog**
- H2: **Feeding a Dog**
- H2: **Exercising a Dog**

c) Write Naturally with Keywords
Keywords are words that people type when searching on Google. Use them naturally, so the content sounds like you're talking to a friend, not like you're repeating the same word over and over.

Example:
Instead of saying "dog care" five times in one paragraph, you could say, "Taking care of a dog includes feeding, exercise, and love."

d) Add Links

Links are like clues that help readers find more information. There are two types:

- **Internal links:** Links to other pages on your website.
- **External links:** Links to other websites with valuable information.

Example:

If you're talking about "dog health tips," you could link to another article on your site about "healthy dog foods" or link to a trusted website like the American Kennel Club.

3. Optimizing for Readability

Readability means writing content that's easy to read and understand.

a) Short Sentences and Paragraphs

Using short sentences helps readers follow along without getting lost. Paragraphs should also be short, usually two to three sentences.

Example:

Instead of:

"Dog training is a process that requires time, patience, and consistency, but with the right approach, you can teach your dog to follow commands and behave well."

Write:

"Training a dog takes time and patience. With the right steps, you can teach your dog to follow commands."

b) Use Bullet Points and Lists

Lists are easier to read than long paragraphs. They let readers quickly see the main points.

Example:

If you're listing the benefits of dog ownership, use bullets:

- Dogs are great friends.
- They help us exercise.
- They make us feel happy.

c) Use Simple Words

Avoid using complex words or too many technical terms. Imagine explaining your topic to a friend or younger sibling.

Example:
Instead of saying "a canine's nutrition," just say "dog food."

4. Optimizing for Engagement

Engagement means creating content that makes people want to stay on the page longer and interact.

a) Add Images or Videos
Images and videos make content more exciting and fun. Pictures of puppies, for instance, can grab attention and make people smile.

Example:
If you're talking about different dog breeds, add pictures of each breed so readers can see what they look like.

b) Use Questions
Asking questions keeps people interested and thinking about what you're saying. It feels like having a conversation.

Example:
Instead of saying, "Dogs need exercise," you could ask, "Did you know dogs need exercise every day?"

c) Add a Call-to-Action (CTA)
A CTA tells readers what to do next, like "click here," "learn more," or "subscribe." It helps guide them through your website.

Example:
At the end of an article about dog training, you might say, "Want more training tips? Check out our full guide on dog training here!"

5. Optimizing for Keyword Relevance

Keyword relevance means using words that match what people are looking for.

a) Use Keywords in the Right Places
Put your main keyword in key places:

- Title: This shows readers and Google what your page is about.
- First paragraph: Using the keyword early helps set the topic.

- Headers and subheaders: Google looks at these to understand the main points.

Example:
If your keyword is "dog training tips," your title might be "Top 10 Dog Training Tips for Beginners," and the first paragraph could say, "Dog training tips help owners teach their dogs good habits."

b) Don't "Stuff" Keywords
Keyword stuffing means using the keyword too much, making content sound unnatural. Google doesn't like this and may rank your page lower.

Example:
Instead of: "Dog training tips are important for dog owners. These dog training tips help with training. Dog training tips should be easy to understand."

Write: "Dog training tips help owners train their dogs effectively. Learning these tips can make training easier and more fun."

c) Use Synonyms and Related Words
Using similar words helps Google understand the topic without needing the exact keyword repeatedly.

Example:

If your keyword is "dog training tips," you can also say "training advice for dogs" or "ways to train your dog."

Final Example Recap: Putting it All Together

Imagine you're writing a blog called "5 Fun Dog Training Tips."

1. **Title:** Use "5 Fun Dog Training Tips" to grab attention and use the keyword.
2. **Headings:** Use headings like "Tip 1: Keep Training Short and Fun."
3. **Readability:** Write short paragraphs, like "Training doesn't have to be long. Just 5 minutes a day is a good start!"
4. **Engagement:** Add a cute picture of a dog fetching a ball.
5. **Keyword Relevance:** Use "dog training tips" in the first paragraph and headers but only where it fits naturally.

By following these steps, you create content that's helpful, easy to find, and fun for people to read!

Lesson 2: Keyword Placement and Density

Welcome to Keyword Fun Land! 🚀 In this lesson, we'll dive into where and how to place keywords in your content and learn the magic balance for keyword density.

That way, we make search engines happy without stuffing in so many keywords that they lose their effect. Let's explore it step by step—plus, we'll throw in some jokes to make it more fun! 😊

What's Keyword Placement? 🎯

Imagine keywords as tiny "road signs" that show search engines what your page is about. But, like with any good road sign, they need to be in the right places to guide search engines correctly! Here's where to put them for the best results.

Title Tag (the Title of Your Page)

- Think of the title as the cover of your book. It should give readers and search engines an idea of what's inside.
- **Example:** If you're writing about "Best Dog Toys," your title could be "Top 10 Best Dog Toys for Every Pup."
- **Why It Works:** Search engines notice keywords in the title and rank it higher if it's clear and relevant.
- **Fun Fact:** Using a keyword in the title can boost rankings by around 20%! 📈

SEO Joke: Why did the SEO expert break up with the website? It just wasn't the *right title*! 😊

Headers (H1, H2, H3)

- Headers act like chapter titles in a book. They break up content, so readers can easily follow along.
- **Example:** If your keyword is "Healthy Snacks for Kids," then an H2 header could be "Why Healthy Snacks Matter" and an H3 could be "Top 5 Yummy and Nutritious Snacks."

- **Why It Works:** Putting keywords in headers signals to search engines that this content is well-organized and helpful, which improves ranking chances.

SEO Joke: How many SEOs does it take to change a light bulb? Just one… but they'll try to add the keyword "light bulb" at least five times in the header! 😄

Body Content (The Main Text)

- This is where you share all the juicy details! Placing keywords naturally in the body helps search engines confirm your topic.
- **Example:** Let's say your keyword is "Camping Tips for Beginners." A sentence in the body could be: "One of the best camping tips for beginners is to plan meals ahead."
- **Why It Works:** Including keywords in the body content helps search engines see you're providing valuable info on that topic.

Pro Tip: Don't force it! Keywords should blend in naturally with the content so it reads well.

SEO Joke: Why did the SEO copywriter go broke? They kept putting their keywords in the wrong *places*…

☐

Image Alt Text (The Little Descriptions for Images)

- Alt text is a short description for each image on your site. It's essential for accessibility (helping people with visual impairments understand what's in the image) and also helps search engines know what the image is about.
- **Example:** For an image of a mountain sunset, use alt text like "Beautiful mountain sunset view."
- **Why It Works:** When search engines read your alt text, they learn more about the images on your site, which helps rank your page in image searches.

SEO Joke: How did the SEO expert get so rich? They found the *alt-text-er-nate* way to success! ☺

What's Keyword Density? ✸

Keyword density is the number of times your keyword appears in your text, shown as a percentage. For example, if you have a 100-word article and use your keyword five times, your keyword density is 5%.

Best Practices for Keyword Density

- **1-2% is Ideal**: Most SEO experts agree that a 1-2% keyword density is perfect. So, for a 500-word page, aim to include your keyword 5-10 times.
  Example: For a 1000-word page on "Tropical Fish Care," aim for 10-20 uses of that phrase, spread out naturally.

- **Avoid Keyword Stuffing**: Keyword stuffing is when you force keywords into a page too many times. It can make your content sound awkward, and search engines dislike it. Overuse can actually lead to penalties that lower your rankings!

Example: Instead of "Tropical fish care is important for fish health, and tropical fish care involves feeding fish properly," try, "Tropical fish care includes feeding them right, maintaining water quality, and giving them a good habitat."

SEO Joke: Why don't SEOs like too many keywords in one sentence? Because they can't *bear* it! (Keyword *bear*-ing, get it? 😄)

Final Tips on Strategic Keyword Placement and Density

1. **Use Synonyms and Variations**: Keywords don't have to be exactly the same every time. Using variations helps avoid repetition and sounds more natural.
   - **Example**: If your keyword is "Best Cat Food," you could also say "Top Food for Cats" or "Healthy Cat Meals."
   - **Why It Works**: Search engines understand synonyms, so this can help

your ranking without overusing one keyword.

2. **Spread Keywords Naturally**: Don't just stack all your keywords at the top or bottom—spread them out across your text, like a nice sprinkling of salt.
   - **Example:** Instead of mentioning "Organic Gardening Tips" ten times in one paragraph, aim for a couple of mentions in each section of the content.

3. **Add Value to Readers**: Always remember, writing should be for people first, search engines second. When your content is valuable and informative, it naturally attracts readers (and search engines).
   SEO Joke: How did the SEO become popular? They knew how to *place* themselves right! 😄

A Quick Recap 📝

- **Keyword Placement** is all about using your keyword in specific areas: title, headers, body, and alt text.
- **Keyword Density** is the frequency of your keyword, ideally around 1-2% of your total content.
- **Avoid Keyword Stuffing**: It's better to sound natural than to overdo it!

Remember: Good SEO is like making a delicious soup. A little salt (keywords) enhances the flavor, but too much ruins the dish! ☺

Final SEO Joke: Why did the SEO writer go to therapy? They couldn't stop *placing* their feelings in every sentence! 😄

Lesson 3: Meta Tags Optimization (Title Tags, Meta Descriptions)

Introduction to Meta Tags

Imagine you're at a big party with tons of people, and you want everyone to notice you. You wear a cool badge that says, "Hi, I'm [Your Name], I'm fun, and I have the best jokes!"

Now, people know a little about you before even talking to you. That's exactly what **meta tags** do for websites! They give a quick preview of what a web page is all about.

Importance of Title Tags and Meta Descriptions

Meta tags, especially **title tags** and **meta descriptions**, act like tiny invitations to visit a web page. Here's how they help:

- **Title Tags**: Think of these as the headline of a story. They give the main idea of what your page is about, so search engines like Google know if it's relevant to people's searches.

- **Meta Descriptions**: This is like the summary on the back of a book. It gives a short description of your page's content, which helps people decide if they want to click and read more.

  SEO Joke: Why did the web page bring a ladder to the party?
  Answer: To improve its "ranking"! 😄

Why Do Title Tags and Meta Descriptions Matter?

- **Catchy Clicks**: A well-crafted title and description can make people want to click on your link.
- **Better Rankings**: Good meta tags help search engines know your content is valuable, which can help it appear higher in search results.
- **Standing Out**: With so many search results, a creative title or description can make your link shine brighter than others!

  Pro Tip 💡: Keep title tags around **50-60 characters** so they display fully on search engines!

Crafting Effective Title Tags

A great title tag is like a superhero costume—it grabs attention, says who you are, and makes people want to see more.

Steps to Create a Perfect Title Tag

1. **Use Your Keywords**: If your page is about "puppy training," make sure those words are in the title! Search engines need keywords to know what the page is about.
   - **Example**: Instead of "How to Train Your Pet," try "Puppy Training: Easy Steps for Happy Puppies!"

2. **Be Specific**: Make sure people know exactly what they're getting when they click.
   - **Example**: "Puppy Training Tips" is nice, but "10 Puppy Training Tips for Beginners" is even better!

3. **Keep It Short and Sweet**: A title tag should be between 50-60 characters. Anything longer might get cut off on search results.
    - **Example**: "Learn How to Train Your Puppy in 7 Days or Less" is better than a long title like "Learn How to Train Your Puppy, Stop Them From Barking, and Make Them Listen in Just 7 Days!"

4. **Make It Catchy**: Imagine your title as a movie trailer—make people curious!
    - **Example**: "Puppy Training Made Easy—Unlock the Secrets Today!" adds a bit of excitement.

   Pro Tip 💡: Try starting with action words like "Learn," "Discover," or "Get Tips" to make it more inviting!

Writing Clickable and Optimized Meta Descriptions

Your meta description is the invitation card for your website. It should tell people why they'll love your page, making them curious enough to click.

Steps to Create an Awesome Meta Description

1. **Use Keywords Naturally**: Keywords help search engines, but they also reassure users that your page covers what they're looking for.
   - **Example**: For a puppy training page, try "Discover easy puppy training tips to make your new friend happy and well-behaved."

2. **Include a Call-to-Action**: Encouraging people to take action, like "Learn more" or "Find out now," makes them more likely to click.
   - **Example**: "Learn the top puppy training secrets! Click to make training fun and easy."

3. **Keep It Between 150-160 Characters**: Too long, and the description will get cut off. Too short, and it may not give enough info.
    - **Example**: "Get tips to train your puppy and build a stronger bond—simple steps anyone can follow!"

4. **Highlight Benefits**: Tell readers what's in it for them.
    - **Example**: "Say goodbye to messes! These puppy training tips make life easier and keep your pup happy."

SEO Joke: Why did the SEO specialist bring a flashlight?
Answer: To fix their "meta-darkness"! 😄

Example Meta Descriptions

1. **Short and Sweet**: "Need puppy training tips? Get the best tricks for happy, well-behaved puppies."

2. **Detailed with Benefits**: "Learn how to train your puppy in a week! Easy tips to keep your furry friend on their best behavior."
3. **With a Call-to-Action**: "Discover the top 5 puppy training secrets today—click to make training easy and fun!"

Pro Tip 💡: Use power words like "best," "top," and "easy" to make your description pop!

Why Well-Crafted Meta Tags Make a Difference

Meta tags are powerful for SEO because they directly impact:

- **Click-Through Rates (CTR)**: More people clicking on your link tells Google your page is valuable, which could help with ranking!
- **User Experience**: When titles and descriptions match your content, users are more likely to stay on your page.

- **Competitive Edge**: A catchy meta tag can give you an advantage over other pages that might seem dull or unclear.

Fun Data: Meta Tags in Numbers

Did you know?

- Pages with well-optimized title tags can have up to **20% higher click-through rates**!
- Keeping meta descriptions relevant and concise can increase user satisfaction by **35%**.

    SEO Joke: What does an SEO do with broken links?
    Answer: They call it a "URL cry-sis"! ☺

Wrapping Up: Key Takeaways

1. **Title Tags** should be short, catchy, and keyword-rich. They're the headline that grabs attention.

2. **Meta Descriptions** should invite users in, give a taste of your content, and include a call-to-action.
3. **Don't Overstuff Keywords**: Just like adding too many sprinkles on ice cream, too many keywords can ruin the experience.
4. **Test and Tweak**: Meta tags can always be improved. Check analytics to see what works best.

Pro Tip 💡: Update your meta tags regularly to keep them fresh and relevant!

Now you know how meta tags can make a big impact on getting people to visit your site! So go ahead, add some sparkle to your title tags and meta descriptions—and watch the clicks roll in!

Lesson 4: Header Tags (H1, H2, H3)

Using Headers to Improve Content Structure and SEO

Headers, like H1, H2, and H3, work like labels in a book that help organize the content so it's easier to read and understand. Think of them as signs that guide readers and search engines, showing what's most important and what's connected. Each header has a job to do! Just like we have book titles, chapter names, and section titles, headers in SEO help content flow smoothly. So, let's dive into how headers help your content shine and rank higher on search engines.

Why Are Headers Important?

Headers tell search engines what's important on a page, which helps them decide how to rank your content.

Good headers make your content look neat and organized, like putting your clothes in drawers instead of leaving them all over the floor! ☺ Search engines like Google see these headers as signals, saying, "Hey, this part is important; check it out!" And when your page is well-organized, readers are more likely to stick around.

Example: Imagine writing about "Healthy Snacks for Kids." You could structure it like this:

- **H1: Healthy Snacks for Kids**
  - **H2: Easy Snacks to Make at Home**
    - **H3: Fruits and Veggies**
    - **H3: Sandwich Ideas**
  - **H2: Snacks for School Lunches**
    - **H3: Nut-Free Options**
    - **H3: Protein-Packed Snacks**

With this setup, readers know where to find what they need, and search engines understand the main topic and subtopics.

SEO Joke:
Why did the webpage get promoted?
Because it knew how to "header" itself to the top! 😊

Pro Tip 💡:
Keep your headers short and sweet—no need to make them too long. Headers are here to summarize, not tell the whole story!

Proper Use of H1 Tags: The Main Title

The H1 tag is like the book title. It's the big, bold statement that tells everyone what the page is about. You should only have one H1 per page, just like a book usually has one main title.

Example: If your page is about "How to Care for Houseplants," the H1 would simply be:

- **H1: How to Care for Houseplants**

An H1 tag grabs attention, so make sure it's clear and matches what the page is all about. Also, it's one of the first things search engines look at, so including your main keyword here is super helpful.

SEO Joke:
How does an H1 tag stay in shape?
By keeping its content lean and focused! 😊

Pro Tip 💡:
Make your H1 tag unique and interesting—stand out from the crowd! Instead of saying "Dog Training Tips," say "Top Dog Training Tips for a Happy Pup!"

Using H2 Tags: The Main Sections

H2 tags act as chapter titles or main sections within your content. They help break down the content into parts that are easy to understand, like sorting your clothes into pants, shirts, and socks! H2s help readers jump to what they care about most without reading the entire page.

Example: For a page about "How to Train a Puppy," you might use H2s like this:

- **H1: How to Train a Puppy**
  - **H2: Basic Puppy Commands**
  - **H2: Potty Training Tips**
  - **H2: Teaching Good Behavior**

This setup helps readers find the specific sections they're interested in. H2 tags also help search engines understand the main topics covered in your content.

Pro Tip 💡:
Make sure your H2 tags are descriptive but not too

long! Use keywords if they fit naturally, like "Healthy Snack Ideas" instead of just "Snacks."

Proper Use of H3 Tags: Subsections

H3 tags work as subpoints under H2 headers, like a list of steps for each topic. H3 tags help organize the smaller details that make up each main idea, making the information easy to scan.

Example: Going back to our "Healthy Snacks for Kids" example, here's how H3 tags would look:

- **H1: Healthy Snacks for Kids**
  - **H2: Easy Snacks to Make at Home**
    - **H3: Fruits and Veggies**
      (Here, you could talk about specific fruits like apples, bananas, etc.)
    - **H3: Sandwich Ideas**
      (Here, you could list different sandwich ingredients.)

Using H3s to divide each topic keeps the content well-organized for readers and helps search engines see how detailed your content is. It's like adding little bookmarks within each chapter so readers can go straight to the info they need.

SEO Joke:
Why did the webpage get so many clicks?
It nailed the "header" game! 😊

Pro Tip 💡:
Think of H3s as a way to add extra detail without overwhelming the reader. They're like bonus info for anyone who wants to dive deeper.

Header Tags and SEO: How They Work Together

When you use headers correctly, search engines notice how well-organized and helpful your content is. It's like showing them a map of what's on your page! Headers make it easier for Google and other search engines to understand what's important, which boosts your SEO ranking.

In fact, studies show that pages with clear, well-organized headers perform better in search results because both people and search engines can quickly see what the page is about. So, using headers the right way is one of the simplest ways to improve your SEO.

Example:
Imagine you're reading an article titled "Best Hiking Trails for Beginners." If it's just a big block of text, you'll probably get bored and leave. But if it has headers like "Trail Preparation," "Top Beginner Trails," and "Hiking Safety Tips," you'll know exactly where to find what you're looking for!

SEO Joke:
What do headers love at work?
Getting promoted to the top of the page! 😄

Pro Tip 💡:
Always check your headers to ensure they follow a logical order—no skipping from H1 to H3 without an H2 in between!

Common Mistakes with Headers

1. **Using Multiple H1 Tags:** Only one H1 per page! Imagine a book with two titles—confusing, right?
2. **Skipping Header Levels:** Headers should follow a hierarchy (H1 > H2 > H3).
3. **Keyword Stuffing in Headers:** Don't cram keywords into every header. Keep it natural!
4. **Making Headers Too Long:** Remember, headers are guides, not paragraphs!

Example of Good Practice:

- **H1: Learn to Bake a Cake**
  - **H2: Ingredients Needed**
    - **H3: Basic Ingredients**
    - **H3: Optional Add-ins**
  - **H2: Steps to Make the Cake**
    - **H3: Mixing the Batter**
    - **H3: Baking Time and Tips**

SEO Joke:
What's a header's favorite song?
"I'm on top of the page!" 😊

Pro Tip 💡:
Check your headers on mobile devices. Sometimes, what looks good on a computer screen can look squished or overwhelming on a phone!

Wrapping Up: Headers for Structure and SEO

Headers aren't just for looks—they help organize your content, improve readability, and boost SEO. A well-structured page is easier for readers to enjoy and for search engines to rank higher.

So, when you're creating content, think of headers as a helpful roadmap. With H1 as your main title, H2s as major sections, and H3s as detailed points, you'll keep everyone happy—from search engines to readers!

Final SEO Joke:
Why did the SEO expert use so many headers?
They knew it was the "write" way to rank! 😄

Pro Tip 💡:
Always keep your headers clear and relevant. A well-

organized page is a happy page—both for readers and search engines!

Lesson 5: Image Optimization and Alt Text

1. Why Are Images Important for User Experience?

Imagine you're reading a storybook with no pictures. It might get boring, right? ☐ Pictures make things fun and exciting!

The same goes for websites. Images keep visitors interested and make them feel like, "Wow, this site knows what I want!" That's why images are essential for a good user experience.

Example:
Think of a cooking website. You go there to learn how to make chocolate chip cookies ☺, and it shows you a picture of warm, gooey cookies fresh from the oven. Now, you're excited to make them yourself! That picture gives you a better idea of what your cookies should look like.

Pro Tip 💡: Use high-quality images to make your website look professional. Blurry pictures? Not cool! 📷

SEO Joke 😄:
Why did the picture file fail SEO school?
It couldn't *"fit in the frame!"*

---

2. Optimizing Images (Making Them Faster and More Searchable)

Did you know images can be *too big*? Yep! Imagine you want to download a photo, but it takes forever. That's what happens when images aren't optimized! Let's learn how to make images faster and searchable with a few steps.

Step 1: Shrink the File Size ✏️

When images are huge, they slow down your website. Big images are like trying to squeeze a giant teddy bear ☐ into a tiny box—it doesn't fit well! Smaller file sizes help websites load faster, which makes visitors (and Google) happier.

Example:

Say you have a photo that's 5 MB (that's really big!).
By resizing it to 500 KB (that's smaller!), it still looks
great on the website but loads much faster.

Pro Tip 💡: Use tools like TinyPNG or ImageOptim to
shrink images without losing quality.

Step 2: Adding Alt Text (Describing the Image)

Alt text is like a hidden description of an image, written
in words. Why do we need it? Some people use
screen readers that read websites out loud, especially
if they can't see well.

Alt text tells them what each image is about, so they
don't miss out on important details. Google also uses
alt text to understand images better and rank websites.

Example:

Let's say you have a picture of a puppy chasing a
butterfly 🐶□. A good alt text could be: "Golden
Retriever puppy chasing a butterfly in a garden." This

way, anyone who can't see the image still knows what it's about!

Pro Tip 💡: Make alt text simple and clear, and don't just write "image" or "picture." Google wants to know *what* the picture is!

SEO Joke 😄:
Why was the image sad?
Because its *alt text* didn't describe its beauty! 😄

Step 3: Add Captions When Needed

Captions are the text that appears right under an image, explaining what's going on in the picture. While not every image needs a caption, it's useful when you want to give a bit more info to your readers. Captions help people understand the picture better and spend more time on your website, which is great for SEO!

Example:
Imagine a picture of a group of kids playing soccer. A caption like "Kids having fun at a weekend soccer game in the park" gives context to the image.

Pro Tip 💡: Use captions when you have something valuable to add. But don't add captions to every image—only when it makes sense.

Fun Fact: Sites with captions under images often get more attention from readers, which makes your page look *extra* interesting to search engines like Google!

---

3. How Image Optimization Helps SEO

When images are fast, have good alt text, and are interesting to look at, Google thinks, "Hey, this website is helpful!" Here's why image optimization is key to SEO:

- **Faster Loading = Happy Visitors:** Fast-loading websites keep visitors from clicking away, and Google loves websites that keep people around.
- **Alt Text = Better Search Ranking:** Google can't see images, but it can read alt text. If your alt text includes a relevant keyword (like "chocolate chip cookies" for a cookie recipe site), it can help your page rank higher.

- **Better User Experience = More Time on Site:**
  When people like what they see, they stay
  longer, click around, and Google thinks your
  site is awesome!

Example:
Imagine a website for a hiking trail with images of
beautiful mountain views ⬜⬜. If those images are
optimized, the site loads faster, people see amazing
pictures, and they're more likely to stay on the site
longer. Google notices this, and that site might even
rank higher!

SEO Joke 😊:
Why did the image take a nap?
It was *too slow* and needed to *refresh!* 😊

---

4. How to Do It: A Step-By-Step Guide

1. **Resize Your Images:** Use tools like TinyPNG
   or Adobe Photoshop to make images smaller.
2. **Write Descriptive Alt Text:** Think of what the
   picture is about and describe it in a few words.

3. **Add Captions (If Needed):** If the image needs extra info, add a short caption to help readers.
4. **Save in the Right Format:** JPEG is good for most photos, PNG works best for logos or images with a transparent background.

Example:
Suppose you have a blog post about "fun summer beach activities." You could:

- Add a picture of kids playing beach volleyball and name it "kids-playing-volleyball-beach.jpg" (not "IMG1234.jpg").
- Write alt text like, "Kids playing volleyball on a sunny beach day."
- Add a caption: "Enjoying a game of volleyball under the sun!"

---

5. Data Snapshot: Why Image Optimization Matters

- **Pages with optimized images load up to 53% faster** than those with large, unoptimized images.

- **Alt text improves search visibility** by up to 15% for image searches on Google.
- **Captions are read 300% more often** than the main body of text. People love a quick explanation right under a picture!

SEO Joke 😄:
Why did the image file become a detective?
Because it *wanted to be found* by search engines!

Summary

Image optimization may seem like a small detail, but it's powerful! Making images faster and giving them the right descriptions helps your website shine in search results. Plus, it creates a better experience for everyone who visits your site. Just remember these steps:

- **Resize images** to load faster.
- **Add alt text** to describe images.
- **Use captions** if they add value.
- **Save in the right format** for web use.

Pro Tip 💡: Don't skip image optimization! A well-optimized site looks better, ranks higher, and makes visitors want to come back.

With images that are well-optimized, your website can rank higher, attract more visitors, and create a fantastic experience for everyone. Remember, every picture is worth a thousand clicks… when done right! □

Lesson 6: Internal Linking and Site Structure

In this lesson, we're going to learn all about "internal linking" and why having a good "site structure" is like having a well-organized room.

When our website is organized and easy to explore, it helps both people and search engines (like Google) find their way around, just like when our room is tidy!

What is Internal Linking?

Imagine you're on a treasure hunt ⬜🗺️⬜. Internal links are like little clues (or hints) leading you from one page to another on the same website. These links are there to help people keep exploring! For search engines, these links are super important because they help Google understand what pages are most important and which ones are connected.

Example: Let's say you're on a cooking website. If you're reading about "How to Make Pizza" 🍕, an internal link could guide you to another page on the site about "Making the Perfect Tomato Sauce." This way, you keep exploring related topics that are part of the same website!

> **SEO Joke** 😄: Why did the webpage bring a map to the website? Because it didn't want to get lost in the links!

Why is Internal Linking Important?

Internal links do two important things: they help people find what they're looking for, and they give "authority" (or importance) to certain pages. Think of authority as the amount of respect or attention a page gets from search engines.

When we link to a page many times, it tells search engines, "Hey, this page is important!" So, if your pizza page is super important, you'll want to link to it from different places on your site to help search engines (and people) notice it.

Example: On an e-commerce website, if the "Best-Selling Shoes" page is important, you might link to it from pages like "Popular Items," "Latest Trends," or "Shoes for All Seasons." This helps search engines know that your "Best-Selling Shoes" page matters a lot.

> **Pro Tip** 💡: Make sure not to link every single word to another page, or it can feel like too much! Just link the pages you really want people (and search engines) to see.

Building an Effective Internal Linking Structure

An internal linking structure is like having a treasure map. Some pages are the "big treasures" that you want people to find, and other pages support them by linking to them.

1. Choose Your Important Pages

Start by choosing which pages are most important. These are the pages you want visitors to see the most. They should have valuable content that is helpful or interesting.

Example: For a website about space, important pages might include "Planets of the Solar System," "Space Missions," or "Astronaut Training."

> **Pro Tip** 💡: Always keep your most important pages easy to find. Think of them as the center of your website's "map."

2. Link Supporting Pages to Important Pages

Supporting pages are the smaller, specific topics. For example, a "Planets of the Solar System" page could have links to smaller pages like "Facts About Mars" or "Why Pluto is No Longer a Planet."

This way, people can keep exploring, and Google understands how the pages are connected.

Example: If you have a page on "Why Vegetables Are Healthy," it could link to supporting pages like "Top 5 Vegetables to Eat" and "Nutrients Found in Green Vegetables."

> **SEO Joke** 😅: Why did the blogger put links on all their pages? Because they wanted to make connections!

3. Use Descriptive Anchor Text

The anchor text is the clickable part of the link, like this: Visit Our Blog. Anchor text should tell people what they'll find on the next page. Avoid using phrases like "click here" as it doesn't explain anything.

Example: Instead of saying "Click here to learn about fruit," say, "Learn more about the benefits of fruit." This way, people know what they're clicking on.

> **Pro Tip** 💡: Descriptive anchor text also helps search engines understand the topic

of the linked page. So, the clearer, the better!

Improving Site Navigation

Site navigation is like having clear signs in a mall. It makes sure people know where they're going and how to get to different areas. This is super helpful for both visitors and search engines.

1. Organize Pages with Categories

Break down your site into categories, so people can explore based on topics. Categories are like sections of a library where similar books are grouped together.

Example: On a travel website, categories could be "Beach Destinations," "Mountain Adventures," and "City Tours." Each category can then link to related pages.

> **SEO Joke** 😅: Why did the web designer break up with the website? It had way too many dead links!

2. Add a Search Bar

Having a search bar on your site is like giving people a "shortcut" to finding exactly what they want. This is especially useful for websites with a lot of content.

Example: Imagine a blog with 200 posts. If someone wants to read only the "Travel" posts, a search bar can make that easy.

> **Pro Tip** 💡: A search bar doesn't just help people—it helps search engines find content and understand your site better!

Distributing Authority Throughout Your Site

Authority isn't just for the main pages. You can help all your pages get some attention (authority) by linking to them. This is called distributing authority, and it's like sharing the love!

1. Link from Popular Pages to Newer Pages

If you have popular pages that get a lot of visitors, link to newer or less popular pages from there. It helps Google know that these newer pages are also worth visiting.

Example: If your "Homemade Pizza Recipe" page is popular, link it to your new "Pizza Topping Ideas" page. This way, the new page gets some attention too.

> **SEO Joke** 😊: Why did the website get into trouble? Because it couldn't link to good behavior!

2. Create a "Related Pages" Section

Adding a "Related Pages" section at the end of each article keeps people exploring, and it shares authority with those linked pages. It's like saying, "Hey, if you liked this, you might enjoy these too!"

Example: If you have a post about "Benefits of Exercise," you can add links at the end to pages like "How to Start a Workout Routine" and "Best Exercises for Beginners."

Pro Tip 💡: Use this section thoughtfully to connect related content. It keeps people on your site longer, which is great for SEO!

Wrapping It Up

Just like organizing your room makes it easier to find things, organizing your website with a good internal linking structure and easy navigation helps everyone get where they want to go. Plus, search engines give more love to sites that are well-organized.

Quick Recap:

- **Internal Links** help connect pages on your website, guiding visitors to explore.
- **Site Structure** helps people and search engines find important pages.
- **Authority Distribution** is about helping all your pages get some attention.

SEO Joke 😄: Why did the website bring a flashlight to the SEO audit? Because it wanted to shine on all the hidden pages!

By building a good internal linking structure, you're creating a solid "map" that search engines can follow easily. So, let's keep linking like a pro and help both visitors and search engines find all the good stuff on your site!

Lesson 7: User Experience (UX) and SEO

What is User Experience (UX)?

User Experience, or UX, is all about how people feel when they use a website. Imagine you walk into a candy store. If everything is easy to find and the candy looks yummy, you have a great experience! But if the candy is hidden, and the store is messy, you probably won't want to stay long.

In the same way, a website needs to be friendly and easy to use so that visitors have a good time and want to stay. When people have a positive experience on a site, they are more likely to come back, and that helps the site rank better on search engines like Google.

Example:

Think about your favorite game. If it loads quickly and is easy to play, you enjoy it more! But if it takes forever to start, you might close it and play something else.

Role of UX in SEO

1. **Page Speed**
   - Page speed is how fast a website loads. If a website takes too long to open, people will leave and go to a faster site. Google notices this and may lower the website's ranking.
   - **Data Example:** According to Google, if a page takes more than **3 seconds** to load, **53%** of mobile users will leave!
2. **SEO Joke:** Why did the web page break up with the server?
   Because it couldn't handle the load! ☺
3. **Mobile-Friendliness**

- Many people use their phones to browse the internet. If a website doesn't look good on a phone, users will struggle to navigate it.
  - Google looks for mobile-friendly websites and gives them a higher ranking. If your website isn't friendly to mobile devices, it might be like a candy store without any candy for kids!
4. **Pro Tip** 💡**:** You can use tools like Google's Mobile-Friendly Test to see if your site works well on phones.

Example:

If you have a website about animals, and it loads slowly on a phone, kids will get frustrated and go play a game instead. But if it's fast and easy to read on their phone, they'll stay and learn about lions and tigers!

How to Enhance UX to Support SEO Goals

1. **Make It Fast!**

- Use good web hosting and compress images to help your site load faster.
- **Example:** If you have a picture of a cute puppy that is too big, it can slow down the site. Using a smaller version makes it load faster!

2. **Keep It Simple**
   - A clean design helps users find what they are looking for. If they can't find the search button, they might leave.
   - **Example:** Think of your bedroom. If it's messy, you can't find your toys. But if everything is organized, you can quickly find what you want!

3. **SEO Joke:** Why did the SEO expert take a ladder to work?
   Because they wanted to reach new heights in user experience! 😄

4. **Use Clear Navigation**
   - Make sure visitors can easily find different pages. Use menus with clear labels so users don't get lost.
   - **Example:** If your website has sections like "Fun Facts" and "Games," make sure they are easy to see. If visitors

have to search hard, they may get frustrated.

5. **Responsive Design**
   - This means that your website should look good on any device, whether it's a computer, tablet, or phone.
   - **Example:** Imagine if you wore a shirt that was too big! It wouldn't look good, right? A website should fit well on every device.

6. **Pro Tip 💡:** Use a responsive web design tool to make sure your site looks good everywhere!

7. **Engaging Content**
   - Write interesting articles and use images or videos to keep visitors entertained. When people enjoy what they read, they stay longer.
   - **Example:** If you write about space, using fun images of planets will keep kids excited!

8. **Feedback and Improvement**
   - Ask your visitors how they feel about your site. You can use surveys to find out what they like and what they don't.

- Example: If many visitors say your site is confusing, you can fix it, just like cleaning up your messy room!
9. SEO Joke: Why was the website always invited to parties?
   Because it knew how to engage the audience! 😄

Conclusion

User experience (UX) and SEO go hand in hand. When you create a friendly, fast, and easy-to-use website, you not only make visitors happy, but you also help your site rank better on search engines. Remember, a good user experience means more visitors, and more visitors mean more success!

So, let's make sure our websites are like a fun candy store—easy to navigate, quick to load, and full of sweet content that everyone will love!

Now go and enhance your UX, and watch your SEO goals soar! 🚀

With these tips and examples, you're ready to make your website shine! If you have any questions or need help, don't hesitate to ask. Happy optimizing!

Module 4: Off-Page SEO

Lesson 1: What Is Off-Page SEO?

Introduction to Off-Page SEO and Why It Matters

Off-page SEO is like the popularity contest for websites! Imagine you're the coolest kid in school, and everyone wants to be your friend. When your website is popular, search engines like Google think, "This website must be important!" So, they give you a better spot in the search results. Off-page SEO is about getting other websites to "talk" about your website, which helps search engines see that your site is trustworthy and valuable.

> **Example:** Let's say you own a website about pet care. If other websites (like pet supply stores or animal shelters) mention

your website or link back to it, search engines think, "Wow, this pet care site must be really helpful!" So, they move your website up in the rankings.

Why it matters: Just like in real life, when lots of people say good things about you, others start to believe you're awesome. Off-page SEO is how your website builds its reputation online. And a better reputation means more visitors who can see your content or buy your products.

> **SEO Joke:** Why did the SEO expert keep their website single? Because they couldn't find the right match! (Get it? "Match" as in backlinking!)

Differences Between On-Page and Off-Page SEO

On-Page SEO vs. **Off-Page SEO** is like taking care of yourself versus getting compliments from others. In **on-page SEO,** you focus on making your website content great by adding keywords, optimizing titles, and making everything look good. In **off-page SEO,** you focus on getting others to notice how amazing your website is. Let's break it down:

1. **On-Page SEO**:
   - Happens **on** your website.
   - Includes things like **keywords**, **titles**, and **meta descriptions** (those short explanations that show up in search results).
   - It's like dressing nicely and speaking well.
2. **Off-Page SEO**:
   - Happens **outside** your website.
   - It's about **getting links** from other websites, which are called **backlinks**.
   - Think of it as other people recommending you.

Example: Imagine you're a baker. If you decorate your cakes beautifully, that's like on-page SEO because you're focusing on what's in your bakery. But if a food critic writes an article saying your bakery is the best in town, that's like off-page SEO.

Now, more people trust your bakery because someone else said it's awesome!

Pro Tip 💡: Focus on **building relationships** with other websites in your field. These connections can turn into backlinks, which help boost your website's ranking!

Why Backlinks Are Important

Backlinks are the superstar of off-page SEO. When other websites link back to yours, it's like they're giving you a thumbs up! Search engines notice these "thumbs up" and think, "Wow, this site must be important if others are linking to it!"

Data Fact: A study showed that **websites with more backlinks rank higher** in search results. In fact, the top result on Google has **3.8 times more backlinks** than the result in the second position!

Example: Imagine you own a website about learning how to play the guitar. If a famous musician's website links to your site, search engines think, "This must be a good resource!" So, they give your website a higher spot on the results page.

SEO Joke: Why did the backlink go to therapy? It had commitment issues! ☺

Types of Off-Page SEO Tactics

Now that we know what off-page SEO is, let's look at some common ways to do it:

1. **Link Building:** This is the main part of off-page SEO. When other sites link to yours, it's like a "vote" of confidence. It shows that people find your website helpful and want others to visit it. **Example:** Imagine your website is about healthy recipes. If a popular food blog links to your smoothie recipe, it's like they're saying, "Hey, check this out!" Search engines see that link and think your website must be helpful.

2. **Social Media Marketing:** Being active on social media can help people discover your content and share it. While social media doesn't directly affect SEO, it can bring more visitors to your website, which is still super helpful.
   Example: You post a video on TikTok showing a simple cooking hack. If people like it, they might visit your website for more tips. That traffic tells search engines that people enjoy your content.

3. **Guest Blogging:** Writing articles for other websites in your field is a great way to reach new audiences. Plus, you can link back to your website, which helps build more backlinks.
   Example: Let's say you're a dog trainer. You write a guest post for a popular pet blog with tips on training puppies. In that post, you link back to your website, and now readers from that pet blog know about you, too!

   Pro Tip 💡: Not all backlinks are created equal! Getting a backlink from a popular website like a major news site is much more valuable than one from a small blog. Aim for quality links over quantity.

How Search Engines View Off-Page SEO

Search engines use off-page SEO to decide how trustworthy your website is. When other high-quality sites link to you, it's like getting a gold star. However, if you get links from low-quality sites, it's like getting a thumbs-down. That's why it's essential to focus on good-quality backlinks that come from trusted websites.

> **Example:** Imagine your website is about fitness tips. If a big health website links to one of your workout articles, that's a gold star! But if a low-quality site with no clear focus links to you, it might not help you as much in search engine rankings.

> **SEO Joke:** What do SEOs say after building a great backlink? Link you very much! 😄

How to Get Started with Off-Page SEO

Starting with off-page SEO can feel a bit tricky, but here are some easy steps to begin:

1. **Build Relationships in Your Niche**: Connect with other websites and bloggers in your field. They're more likely to link to your site if you're on good terms.
2. **Create Valuable Content**: If you make content that's helpful and unique, others will naturally want to share and link to it.
3. **Be Active on Social Media**: Share your content, interact with followers, and participate in discussions. The more people see your content, the more likely they'll link to it.

   Example: If you run a travel blog, you could write a unique guide on "Hidden Beaches in the Caribbean." If your guide is interesting, travel websites or social media influencers might link to it.

Wrapping Up

Off-page SEO is a powerful tool to show search engines that your website is popular and valuable. While on-page SEO is like tidying up your room, off-page SEO is more about spreading the word that your room is the coolest place to hang out. By earning backlinks and being active outside your site, you can bring more visitors and boost your website's credibility.

> **Pro Tip** 💡: Be patient! Off-page SEO takes time. Building a good reputation doesn't happen overnight, but with persistence, your website will start to rise in the ranks!

> **Final SEO Joke:** Why did the website break up with its backlink? It felt like it was being used just for SEO points! 😊

Lesson 2: Link Building Basics and Best Practices

What is Link Building?

Imagine you're a kid in school, and you have lots of friends who tell everyone how cool you are. The more people talk about you, the more popular you become, right?

That's what link building is for websites. It's like getting "shout-outs" from other websites. When websites link to your site, they tell search engines like Google, "Hey, this website has cool stuff!" The more links (or shout-outs) you get, the more popular and trustworthy you look.

SEO Joke Time:
Why did the SEO expert get kicked out of the party? Because he was building too many "links" in the punch! 😂

How Link Building Works

To make it super simple, think of link building as creating "friendships" with other websites. When a popular website links to your site, it's like a friend recommending you. The more trustworthy or popular that website is, the better it is for you!

- **Example:** If a famous news site like "CoolNews.com" links to your blog, that link has a lot of power. It's like having a superstar say, "Hey, you should check out my friend's site!"
- **Fun Fact:** Sites like Wikipedia and government websites have strong "link power" because they're trusted sources.

Pro Tip 💡: Not all links are equal. Links from trustworthy websites are better than links from unknown ones, just like a recommendation from a teacher holds more weight than a classmate you've never met.

Do's of Link-Building Strategies

1. **Create Great Content**
   If you want people to talk about you, you've got to give them something cool to share. Make your content helpful, interesting, and easy to read.
   - **Example:** A blog post like "Top 10 Fun Facts About Space" might get linked by science websites and blogs because it's interesting and educational.

- **Data:** Studies show that content with lists (like "Top 10..." posts) gets more links because people find them easy to read and share.

2. **Pro Tip 💡:** Think about what your readers might want to share or link to. For example, if your audience loves animals, a guide on "How to Care for Pets" could be a hit!

3. **Reach Out to Relevant Sites**
Try connecting with websites that are similar to yours or cover topics you write about. When you ask nicely, many site owners are happy to link to helpful content.
    - **Example:** If you write a blog about hiking trails, reach out to an outdoor gear website or a travel blog to share your hiking guide.

4. **SEO Joke Time:**
Why did the link builder break up with the blogger?
Because they didn't "connect" anymore! 😊

5. **Get Listed in Directories**
Online directories are like big phonebooks for the internet. When you get listed there, people (and search engines) find you more easily.

- Example: Websites like Yelp or business directories can link to your website, making it easier for local customers to find you.

6. **Use Social Media for Exposure**
   While social media links don't always count the same as regular links, they're still a good way to show people what you've got. The more people see your site, the more they'll want to link to it.
   - **Example:** Share your latest article on Twitter or Facebook. If people like it, they might link to it from their own blogs or websites.

7. **Pro Tip** 💡**:** Encourage sharing by adding easy-to-click "Share" buttons. The more people see your content, the more links you'll get!

Don'ts of Link-Building Strategies

1. **Don't Buy Links**
   Buying links is like paying people to be your friend. It might work for a short time, but search engines can tell if you're trying to "cheat" the system, and they don't like it.

- Example: If a website suddenly has a lot of purchased links, it might get punished by Google, which could hurt its rankings.

2. **Pro Tip 💡:** Focus on building links naturally by creating great content and connecting with relevant sites. Slow and steady wins the SEO race!

3. **Don't Link to Untrustworthy Sites**
Imagine being friends with someone who's always getting in trouble. It doesn't look great for you, right? Linking to shady or untrustworthy sites can make your website look bad too.
    - Example: If a site links to a lot of spammy sites, search engines might see it as untrustworthy.

4. **Don't Use Too Many Links**
It's good to link to other sites, but if your site is overloaded with links, it might look suspicious or annoying to readers.
    - Example: A blog post with every other word linked can look spammy and isn't fun to read.

5. **SEO Joke Time:**
Why did the SEO expert put fewer links in his article?

Because he didn't want to "break" his readers!
😄

6. **Don't Copy Content Just for Links**
   Search engines value originality, so if you copy
   and paste from other sites, it doesn't look good.
   Focus on being unique and sharing your own
   ideas!
   - **Example:** A travel blog might create
     original guides instead of copying
     others, making it more link-worthy and
     trustworthy.
7. **Pro Tip** 💡: Writing unique, high-quality content
   is the best way to attract natural links. Think of
   it as showing off your own art instead of
   hanging up someone else's painting.

Link-Building Best Practices

- **Be Patient**
  Building links takes time. Think of it as planting
  a garden – you need to water and nurture it
  before seeing results.
  - **Example:** A blog about gardening might
    take months to gather links from other

gardening blogs, but over time, the
trustworthiness builds up.
- **Focus on Quality Over Quantity**
It's better to have a few links from trustworthy
sites than a bunch of links from random or low-
quality sites.
  - ○ **Example:** A single link from a top blog
    in your industry is more valuable than
    50 links from unknown sites.

Final Pro Tip 💡: Link building is like making friends –
find sites that like the same stuff as you, be friendly,
and help each other grow. This way, you'll build
connections that benefit both of you and make your
website stronger.

Lesson 3: Types of Backlinks and Their Value

Welcome to Lesson 3, where we'll explore the world of
backlinks! Backlinks are links from other websites that
point to your website, kind of like a friend vouching for
you.

But not all backlinks are created equal. Today, we'll learn the differences between high-quality and low-quality backlinks, how to assess their value, and why they matter in the SEO world. Get ready for a fun and educational ride!

---

1. Understanding Backlinks: What Are They?

Imagine you're in school, and you need someone to recommend you as the best student for a project. If your teacher recommends you, that's a big deal because it's coming from an expert. But if your friend (who sometimes forgets homework) recommends you, it might not carry the same weight. That's how backlinks work too!

- **High-quality backlink**: A link from a well-known and trusted website, like a teacher's recommendation.
- **Low-quality backlink**: A link from an unknown or unreliable site, kind of like a recommendation from someone who doesn't have a good reputation.

SEO Joke 😊: "Why did the backlink get a bad grade in school? Because it wasn't high-quality!"

Pro Tip 💡**:** Quality always beats quantity. Ten good backlinks are better than 100 poor-quality ones!

---

2. Types of Backlinks and Why They Matter

Backlinks come in different types, each with its value. Some help your site's SEO, while others don't do much. Here's a simple breakdown:

a) Editorial Backlinks

These are backlinks that come from articles or blogs naturally. For example, if a blog writes about "Best Sports Shoes," and they mention your shoe website with a link, that's an editorial backlink.

Why They Matter: Editorial backlinks are often high-quality because they come from trusted sources that naturally refer to your website.

Example: A blog called "Top Shoe Picks" writes, "Check out *YourShoeWebsite.com* for the comfiest shoes around!" This is a strong, high-quality backlink.

b) Guest Post Backlinks

When you write an article for another website, you might get a backlink to your site as a thank-you. It's like borrowing someone else's platform to tell people about you!

Why They Matter: These backlinks are valuable if they come from reputable sites. However, if they're from random, unknown sites, they're not as useful.

Example: You write a post for "FitFam Blog" about the benefits of running, and at the end, they link to your site for more shoe options.

c) Directory Backlinks

These are links from directory sites where you can list your business, like an online phonebook. Think of sites like Yelp or Yellow Pages.

Why They Matter: Directories are helpful if they are trusted, but if they're spammy (filled with too many unrelated businesses), they won't add much value.

Example: Listing on a reputable directory like "Best Local Shops" that includes your site under "Best Shoe Stores."

d) Social Media Backlinks

Links from social media platforms like Facebook, Instagram, or Twitter are also backlinks, though they don't have as much SEO power.

Why They Matter: While they don't directly boost SEO, they bring traffic and visibility, which can lead to more people linking to you naturally!

SEO Joke 😊: "Why did the website break up with social media? Because the backlinks just didn't have the same 'SEO spark'!"

---

3. Differences Between High-Quality and Low-Quality Backlinks

Backlinks differ in quality, and search engines like Google can tell the difference. High-quality backlinks are like gold stars for your website, while low-quality ones can even harm your SEO. Here's what makes them different:

High-Quality Backlinks

- **From Trusted Sites:** Links from sites that people already know and trust, like major news sites or top blogs.
- **Relevant to Your Topic:** The site linking to you should be related to your industry. If you sell shoes, a backlink from a fitness blog is better than one from a recipe site.
- **Natural Links:** If someone links to your site because they genuinely like your content, that's a natural link.

Example: A fitness blog links to your running shoe website because they love your product – that's high quality!

Low-Quality Backlinks

- **From Untrusted Sites:** Links from sites that don't have a good reputation or are new and unknown.
- **Unrelated Topics:** If you're selling shoes and a fishing website links to you, it might look suspicious to search engines.
- **Bought or Forced Links:** If you pay for a backlink, it's usually low-quality because Google doesn't favor paid links.

SEO Joke 😂: "Why don't search engines like low-quality backlinks? Because they just don't 'link up'!"

Pro Tip 💡: Always aim for links from trusted and relevant sites to stay on Google's good side!

---

4. How to Assess Backlink Value

To understand if a backlink is valuable, here are a few things to look for:

a) Authority

Authority is like the popularity of a website. Just as people trust well-known experts, Google trusts high-authority websites. If a famous site links to you, that link has high authority.

Example: If *Sports Magazine* links to your shoe site, it's a high-authority link because people know and trust *Sports Magazine.*

b) Relevance

Relevance is about how closely the website's content matches yours. A backlink from a shoe review site is relevant if you're a shoe store.

Example: A fitness blog linking to your running shoes is relevant, while a site about cooking recipes is not as relevant.

c) Traffic

Check if the website linking to you has lots of visitors. High-traffic sites not only give valuable backlinks but can also send potential customers to your site.

Example: A popular sports blog linking to your shoe website might lead visitors who are genuinely interested in your products.

d) Placement on the Page

The spot where your backlink is placed on the page matters too! Links in the main content area are stronger than links in the footer or sidebar.

Example: If your link is in the main article body, it's more valuable than one buried at the bottom of the page.

SEO Joke ☺: "Where did the backlink go to hide? In the footer! Nobody ever finds it there!"

---

5. Checklist for Evaluating Backlinks

Here's a quick checklist to help you assess if a backlink is high-quality:

1. **Is the linking site well-known and trusted?**
2. **Is the backlink on a relevant website?**
3. **Does the linking page get a lot of visitors?**

4. **Is the link in the main content area?**
5. **Is it a natural link, not paid for?**

Pro Tip 💡*:* Run through this checklist for every backlink to make sure they're helping your SEO and not hurting it.

---

6. Why Backlink Quality Matters More Than Quantity

Google and other search engines prefer quality over quantity. Ten backlinks from high-quality sites can be more powerful than a hundred from random sites. So always go for quality!

Example: Imagine you have 10 gold-star backlinks from well-known fitness blogs for your shoe site. They'll boost your SEO way more than 100 backlinks from random, low-traffic sites.

Backlinks are like little votes of confidence for your website, and each one tells Google that your site is worth trusting. Just remember: a few high-quality links from trusted sources are far better than a mountain of low-quality links from unknown sites. So aim for those gold stars, and your SEO will soar!

Happy backlink building! 🎉

Lesson 4: Link Building Strategies (Guest Blogging, Outreach)

Welcome to Lesson 4! Today, we're diving into link-building strategies with a focus on guest blogging and outreach—two super effective ways to earn valuable links and boost SEO. Let's learn how these strategies can bring more visitors to a website and help search engines see it as trustworthy. And, of course, we'll add some SEO jokes and pro tips to keep things fun! 😄

What is Link Building?

Imagine the internet is like a giant spiderweb, and every time a website links to another, it's like a spider connecting two parts of the web. Link building is when websites try to get links from other trusted sites to make their own site stronger and more popular.

Why do we need links? Well, when search engines like Google see that a website has links from other trusted websites, they think, "This website must be helpful or interesting!" That boosts its ranking in search results.

Pro Tip 💡 **:** Think of links as "votes" for your website. The more you get from high-quality websites, the more "popular" you become to search engines!

Guest Blogging: Sharing Your Ideas

Guest blogging is a link-building technique where you write an article for another website. If the website likes it, they publish it with a link back to your site. This helps in two big ways:

1. It shows people what you know about a topic.
2. It gets you a link from a new website, which boosts your website's authority (trustworthiness).

Here's how to start guest blogging:

1. Finding the Right Websites

First, find websites that talk about similar topics to yours. For example, if you're writing about healthy foods, find websites that talk about fitness or cooking.

- **Example:** Suppose you have a website about "Kids' Healthy Recipes." A fitness blog might be a perfect place to publish your "Top 5 Tasty, Healthy Snacks for Kids" article, and link it back to your website.

2. Writing the Article

Once you find the right website, you'll want to write a helpful article with valuable information. Remember to add a link to your website somewhere in the article (usually at the end or in the author's bio).

- **Example:** If you write "5 Super Snacks for Kids" for a guest blog, you might add at the end, "For more tasty kid-friendly recipes, visit my site [link to your website]!"

3. Guest Blogging Success Tips

- **Be Real:** Write something valuable, not just to get a link. People (and search engines) like genuine, useful content.
- **Be Creative:** Think of a catchy title, like "5 Snacks Kids Will Eat (and Not Just Pretend to Like!)."
- **Stay Relevant:** Make sure the topic fits the website and includes a link that makes sense for readers.

SEO Joke 😂**:** Why did the SEO expert write a bad guest post? He wanted to be *de-ranked*! (Just kidding, never do that!)

Outreach: Asking for Links the Right Way

Outreach means reaching out (hence the name!) to other websites and politely asking them for a link. This works best if your website has a really good piece of content they'd want to share.

1. How to Find Link Opportunities

Think about where your content would be helpful. Let's say your website shares tips about pet care. You could find popular pet blogs, vet websites, or animal shelters with blogs that might want to share your articles.

- **Example:** You have an article on "Top 10 Ways to Keep Your Cat Happy." Look for a cat blog and say, "Hey, I've got a helpful article your readers might enjoy!"

2. Writing the Perfect Outreach Email

A great email can make a huge difference. Here's a basic template you can try:

Subject Line: Thought you might like this article!

Email Body:

Hello [Name of Website Owner],

I just read your article on [Topic Related to Your Article], and I loved it! I've written something similar that I think your readers would enjoy. Here's the link: [Your Article Link].

Let me know if you think it's a good fit for your blog. Thanks for considering!

Best,
[Your Name]

Pro Tip 💡: Keep it short and sweet! No one likes reading super long emails.

3. Following Up Politely

Sometimes people might not reply right away. A friendly reminder after a few days can make a difference. Here's a simple follow-up email:

Subject Line: Just checking in ☐

Email Body:

Hi [Name of Website Owner],

Just wanted to check if you had a chance to look at my article on [Topic]. Let me know if it's something you'd like to share with your readers. Thanks again!

Best,
[Your Name]

SEO Joke 😄**:** Why don't SEOs trust guest post emails? Because sometimes they sound too *link-ly*! 😄

Examples of Good Link Building with Guest Blogging and Outreach

Guest Blogging Example

If your website shares nature photography tips, find blogs about photography or outdoor adventure. Write an article like "5 Tips for Stunning Sunrise Photos." You can then add a link at the end saying, "For more photography tips, visit [Your Website]!"

Outreach Example

Suppose you run a website on plant care and wrote an article on "How to Keep Indoor Plants Alive All Year." You could find popular gardening blogs and say, "Hi, I saw your article on [Gardening Topic]. I have a similar article your readers might find useful!"

Measuring Success in Link Building

How do you know if link-building is working? Here are some simple ways:

1. **Check Website Traffic:** Did you see a jump in visitors after guest blogging or outreach? That's a sign it's working!
2. **Look at Backlinks:** Use tools like Google Search Console to see if other websites have started linking to you.

Pro Tip 💡: The more relevant and high-quality links you get, the better! But don't get links from random or spammy sites—search engines won't like it.

Final Thoughts: Be Friendly, Be Genuine

When link building, focus on quality over quantity. One good link from a trusted site is way better than 10 links from unrelated or low-quality sites. Also, be kind and build real relationships. People are more likely to link to your website if they trust you and see your content as valuable.

SEO Joke 😄**:** Why did the SEO expert go to therapy? To *get over* their *link obsession*!

Link building through guest blogging and outreach is like planting seeds. It may take some time to see the results, but with the right care and effort, those links will grow your website's authority and bring in more visitors. Start small, stay polite, and soon enough, you'll be an outreach and guest-blogging pro! 🌱

Lesson 5: Social Media's Role in SEO

How Social Media Influences SEO and Brand Awareness

Why Does Social Media Matter in SEO?

Social media doesn't directly boost SEO rankings like magic, but it helps in some pretty amazing ways! Imagine you have a website about your favorite snacks.

Now, if you share posts about your snacks on social media, people might visit your website to learn more or even buy those snacks. More people visiting your site sends signals to search engines like Google, showing them that your content is popular and helpful!

Example
Let's say you post a yummy picture of your homemade cookies on Instagram with a link to your recipe. Your friends share it, and their friends see it too! Suddenly, tons of people click on the link, visit your website, and Google thinks, "Wow, this cookie recipe must be good!"

Pro Tip 🔦

Post your content consistently on social media! When people recognize and trust your brand, they're more likely to share and visit your site.

Building Brand Awareness with Social Media

Social media is like a megaphone for your brand. Think of it as shouting out to the world about what you do and why you're awesome! The more people who know about you, the more they might look for you online, boosting your brand's visibility and awareness.

Example

Imagine you're running a page called "Treasure of Tasty Tacos." If you consistently post about new taco recipes, people might start searching for "Tasty Taco recipes" on Google. That search traffic strengthens your brand's recognition and helps it pop up more on Google.

SEO Joke 😄

Why did the SEO expert go broke? Because he kept telling everyone to "pay-per-click"!

Pro Tip 💡
Try adding your website link in all your social media bios. It's an easy way to lead people directly to your main site!

Best Practices for Social SEO Synergy

1. Consistent Branding Across All Platforms

Branding is like your personality online. Make sure your profile picture, bio, and style stay consistent across all social media platforms. This builds trust and helps people recognize you, even if they see you on different platforms.

Example
If your profile picture on Facebook is a red logo, keep the same picture on Instagram and Twitter. If your page's bio says "Best DIY Craft Ideas" on one platform, use the same line on others too.

Pro Tip 💡
Use a similar hashtag across all platforms to get

people to recognize your brand. This helps when people search for you on Google or social media!

---

2. Share Quality Content Regularly

When you share content that's useful or entertaining, more people like and share it. Each share can lead new visitors to your website. More visitors mean higher website traffic, which is good for SEO!

Example
If you have a page about kid-friendly science experiments, share a fun experiment once a week. People may start looking forward to your posts, clicking on your website link, and telling others about it!

SEO Joke 😄
What do you call a page with no likes, no shares, and no clicks? Invisible!

Pro Tip 💡
Mix it up with posts, stories, and even videos! A variety of content keeps followers engaged, helping you stay in their minds (and feeds).

3. Engage with Your Audience

Respond to comments, answer questions, and show appreciation for shares. The more you engage, the stronger your online presence becomes. This creates a community that looks out for your content, which can boost both SEO and brand loyalty.

Example
If someone comments, "Love this cookie recipe!" you could reply, "Thanks so much! Which recipe are you planning to try next?" This can encourage more people to join the conversation.

SEO Joke 😄
Why did the SEO bring a ladder to social media? To reach the "top comment!"

Pro Tip 💡
Set aside 10–15 minutes each day to interact with your audience. Just a little time spent engaging can make a big difference!

4. Use Keywords in Your Social Media Content

Keywords aren't only for Google! Including keywords in your social posts (like "easy cookie recipe" or "fun kids crafts") can make it easier for people to find your content on social media and through search engines.

Example
Let's say you're sharing a post about an "easy chocolate chip cookie recipe" on Facebook. Using those keywords in the post title or caption helps people looking for "easy cookie recipes" to find you!

Pro Tip 💡
Keep a list of top keywords you want to use in your posts. This keeps your message focused and helps people connect your posts with your brand's main topics.

---

5. Collaborate with Influencers or Similar Brands

When you work with other popular pages or influencers, they can introduce your content to their followers. This partnership can drive more traffic to your site, which is great for SEO!

Example

If you're running a page about pet care, team up with a popular pet influencer! When they mention or share your website, their followers might visit your site, increasing traffic.

Pro Tip 💡

Don't have influencers in your niche? Team up with a friend who has followers interested in what you offer. Small steps can still make a big difference!

---

6. Track and Adjust Your Social SEO Strategy

Tracking means checking how many people are visiting your site from social media and which posts bring in the most traffic. With this data, you can adjust your strategy to focus on the posts that work best.

Example

If you notice that video posts get more clicks than photo posts, you could start sharing more videos. This way, you're putting more energy into what gets the best results.

SEO Joke 😄

Why don't search engines trust people on social media? Because they're always clicking "like" but never following through!

Pro Tip 💡

Most social media platforms have built-in tools to track views, clicks, and shares. Use these to refine your strategy!

Wrapping Up

Social media and SEO work together like best friends who hype each other up! While social media doesn't directly affect your ranking on Google, it builds a strong presence that can drive traffic, build brand awareness, and boost your online influence. With these practices, you're ready to share, engage, and grow!

Final SEO Joke 😄

What's an SEO's favorite game on social media? "Hide and seek" with keywords!

Lesson 6: Brand Mentions and Online Reputation Management

1. What Are Brand Mentions, and Why Do They Matter?

Brand mentions are when people talk about a brand online. Imagine your brand's name as a superhero—whenever someone says it online, it gets a little more powerful!

These mentions can happen in blog posts, reviews, social media, and even in comments. They're like free shout-outs that can help more people learn about your brand, boosting your *brand's reputation* and improving your SEO.

- **Example**: If someone writes on Twitter, "I love Pizza Planet's cheesy pizza!" that's a brand mention for Pizza Planet.
- **SEO Joke**: Why did the SEO expert get kicked out of the dinner party? Because they kept asking for more mentions! 😄

How Brand Mentions Help SEO
When search engines like Google notice lots of people

talking about a brand online, it signals that this brand is popular and trustworthy. This can help your website appear higher in search results.

Pro Tip 💡: Keep an eye out for mentions on social media, blogs, and review sites. When people mention your brand positively, it's like getting a golden star for SEO!

---

2. The Importance of Online Reputation Management (ORM)

Online Reputation Management, or ORM, means managing what people say about your brand online. Imagine you have a virtual report card that everyone can see, with reviews, comments, and mentions all over the internet.

If the comments are positive, it makes your brand look good and helps attract more customers. If they're negative, though, it could hurt your brand's reputation.

- **Example**: If people say "Pizza Planet's pizza always arrives late" in a review, that could affect how others feel about ordering from them. ORM would be about responding to that comment and making it right, like offering a discount for next time.

Why ORM Is Important for SEO

If there's too much negative talk about a brand, search engines might lower its rank in results, especially if those comments go unanswered. ORM helps keep the brand's image strong, ensuring search engines and people view it positively.

Pro Tip 💡: Always respond to reviews politely, even if they're negative. Show that you're listening, which builds trust and makes people (and search engines!) like your brand more.

---

3. How to Track Brand Mentions: Useful Tools

Tracking brand mentions helps you know when someone's talking about your brand online. Here are some fun tools that can help:

- **Google Alerts**: This free tool lets you set up alerts for your brand name or keywords.

Whenever your brand name pops up on the web, you'll get an email alert.

- o **Example**: Set up a Google Alert for "Pizza Planet" and get an email when someone mentions it in an article or review.
- **Mention.com**: This tool monitors social media, blogs, news sites, and forums for brand mentions. It's like having an online detective who's always on the lookout!
- **Pro Tip** 💡: Set alerts for common misspellings of your brand too! Sometimes people don't type it correctly, but it's still a valuable mention.

SEO Joke: How did the brand know they were mentioned? Because they had Google Alerts—alerting them everywhere! 😄

---

4. Responding to Positive Brand Mentions

It's always nice when people say good things about your brand. Responding to these mentions shows you're paying attention and appreciate the support. It also helps keep people engaged with your brand!

- **Example**: If someone tweets, "Just had the best pizza from Pizza Planet!" reply with something like, "Thanks for the love! Glad you enjoyed it! 🍕💖"

Responding to positive mentions makes people feel valued and keeps the conversation going. Search engines see this engagement and view your brand as active and well-loved, which can improve your rankings.

Pro Tip 💡: A quick "Thank you!" goes a long way! Engaging with positive mentions can turn happy customers into loyal fans who spread the word.

---

5. Handling Negative Brand Mentions: Keeping Calm and Cool

Sometimes people might say not-so-great things about your brand, and it's crucial to handle these comments carefully. Ignoring them can hurt your online reputation, while responding politely can show you care.

- **Example**: If someone posts, "Pizza Planet forgot my extra cheese," respond by saying, "We're sorry to hear that! Please message us, and we'll make it right for you next time!"

When you respond to negative mentions, it shows that you care about customers. This can even turn a negative experience into a positive one, which helps your reputation and may encourage people to come back.

Pro Tip 💡: Never get into an argument online; a calm, friendly response can make a huge difference! Show empathy, apologize if needed, and offer to help.

SEO Joke: Why did the pizza place never respond to online complaints? Because they thought "no news is good news"—but search engines don't agree! 😊

---

6. ORM Tools for Managing Your Reputation

Besides tracking mentions, you can use ORM tools to monitor and manage your brand's reputation. Here are a few examples:

- **Reputology**: This tool is great for keeping track of reviews on sites like Yelp, Google, and Facebook. It lets you know when there's new feedback, so you can respond quickly.
- **Brandwatch**: With Brandwatch, you can see the bigger picture, monitoring mentions, trends, and customer sentiment to help understand how people feel about your brand overall.
- **Pro Tip** 💡: Use these tools to analyze what people are saying most often. If there's a recurring issue, it may be something worth fixing to keep your customers happy!

SEO Joke: How did the SEO expert check their reputation? By asking "Reputology"—it's their version of a crystal ball! 😊

---

7. Creating Positive Brand Mentions: Encourage Happy Customers to Share

To get more positive brand mentions, sometimes all you need to do is ask! Encourage your happy customers to leave a review or share their experience online.

- **Example**: After a successful order, Pizza Planet could add a note saying, "Loved your pizza? Let us know with a review! 🍕"

This small reminder can help boost positive mentions, which can improve your SEO and reputation over time. The more good things people say about your brand, the more likely search engines will see it as trustworthy.

Pro Tip 💡: Always be polite when asking for reviews, and make it easy for customers to leave one. A simple link to the review page works wonders!

---

8. Keeping Track of Your Reputation: Use Data to Improve

Use the data from mentions and reviews to improve your brand. If many customers praise a certain product, you know what to keep emphasizing. If there are recurring complaints, it's time to fix those issues.

- **Example**: If multiple reviews say "Pizza Planet has the best cheese pizza," highlight that on your website as a customer favorite. If complaints mention slow delivery, focus on improving your delivery speed.

By paying attention to these patterns, you can make better decisions for your brand, helping both your reputation and your SEO.

Pro Tip 💡: Always keep an eye on customer feedback. Trends can help you stay ahead in the game by continuously improving!

In Summary
Brand mentions and online reputation management are crucial for SEO because they build trust and show search engines that people love your brand.

Using tools like Google Alerts, Mention.com, and ORM tools can help you stay on top of what people say about your brand online.

Responding to both positive and negative mentions keeps your brand looking great, which is a win for both customers and SEO!

Final SEO Joke: Why was the SEO expert such a good listener? Because every mention counted! 😊

Module 5: Technical SEO

Lesson 1: Introduction to Technical SEO and Its Importance

What is Technical SEO?

Imagine you have a favorite playground you love to visit. Now, if the playground is full of rocks, broken swings, and messy paths, it wouldn't be as fun, right?

The same goes for websites! Technical SEO is like cleaning up a website's "playground" so it's easier for search engines (like Google) to find, understand, and show it to people searching for something.

Technical SEO helps make sure the website is smooth, fast, and free of issues that could make it hard for search engines to see how cool it is. It's all about the *behind-the-scenes* parts that help a website work perfectly.

SEO Joke:
Why did the website get lost?
Because it didn't have a *map* for search engines to
follow! 😄

Why is Technical SEO Important?

Imagine you make the best lemonade in town, but
you're hidden in a maze with no signs. People would
have trouble finding you, right? Technical SEO is like
putting up signs to make sure everyone can find your
lemonade stand—or, in this case, your website!

When technical SEO is done right:

- Websites load fast, like quick lemonade
  service.
- People can find what they need easily.
- It tells search engines, "Hey, this is a well-kept
  website! Show it to more people!"

Example:
Say you own a website about fun dog facts. Without
technical SEO, it might take ages to load, or search
engines might struggle to find your pages on "Why

Dogs Wag Their Tails." With technical SEO, it's like paving a straight path for both users and search engines to find all the great dog facts on your site.

Common Technical SEO Issues to Address

1. Site Speed: Making It Fast!

Just like a speedy car is more fun to ride, a fast website is more fun to browse. Site speed means how quickly your website loads when someone clicks on it. If it's too slow, people might leave and never come back!

- **Example:** Imagine clicking a website about "The Top 10 Roller Coasters in the World," but it takes 15 seconds to load. You'd probably leave to find another site that's faster, right? That's why speed matters!
- **Pro Tip 💡:** Compress your images! This makes them smaller, so they load faster without taking up too much space.

SEO Joke:
Why did the website take so long to load?
It kept stopping to ask for *directions*! 😊

2. Mobile-Friendliness: Works on Phones, Too!

More than half of all searches come from mobile devices like phones or tablets. So, a website needs to look and work well on a small screen. Mobile-friendly sites adjust automatically, so they're easy to read and click on without any "zooming in."

- **Example:** Imagine you're on your phone and trying to read an article on "How Cats See the World." If the words are tiny and buttons don't work, you might give up. Mobile-friendliness means it's easy to see and use, even on a small screen.
- **Pro Tip 💡:** Use a mobile-friendly test tool to see if your website is easy to use on phones and tablets!

SEO Joke:
Why do websites love mobile users?
Because they keep things *small* and *simple*! 😊

3. Broken Links: Keeping the Path Clear!

Broken links are links that don't go anywhere—like a door that leads to nowhere! When people click on these links, they get a "404 error," which is like saying, "Oops, page not found." Fixing broken links is a big part of technical SEO because they can frustrate users and send them away.

- **Example:** You have a page on "Fun Turtle Facts," and it links to "How Turtles Hide in Their Shells," but that page doesn't work anymore. Fixing or removing the link keeps everything flowing smoothly.
- **Pro Tip 💡:** Use tools to find and fix broken links regularly. It keeps your website tidy and frustration-free.

SEO Joke:
Why did the link break up with the web page?
Because it *wasn't going anywhere!* 😊

4. XML Sitemap: The Website's Treasure Map

An XML sitemap is a list of all the important pages on your website. It's like a treasure map for search engines, showing them where all the best "treasures" are. When search engines know where to go, they can find your pages faster and show them in search results.

- **Example:** Let's say your website has 50 pages about "Cooking Tips." If you make an XML sitemap, it's like telling Google, "Here are all my pages on cooking tips. Go check them out!"
- **Pro Tip 💡:** Create an XML sitemap and submit it to search engines like Google. It's like saying, "Come explore!"

SEO Joke:
What's a search engine's favorite treasure?
A *well-mapped* website! 😊

5. Robots.txt File: Telling Search Engines Where to Go

The robots.txt file is like a signpost at the entrance of a website. It tells search engines where they can or can't go on your website. This helps search engines focus only on the pages you want to show off.

- **Example:** Imagine you have private pages on your site for "Members Only Cooking Recipes." You can use the robots.txt file to say, "Search engines, please don't look at these pages."
- **Pro Tip 💡:** Use robots.txt wisely! Block only the pages you truly don't want search engines to find, like private pages or unimportant sections.

SEO Joke:
What did the robots.txt file say to Google?
"Keep out of my *closet*! 😆

Summary: Why Fixing These Issues Matters

Fixing technical SEO issues makes your website friendlier for both visitors and search engines. When it's easy to use, people will stay longer and come back more often, and search engines will see it as a valuable site, showing it to more people in search results. It's like building a playground that's safe, clean, and fun for everyone to enjoy!

Recap:

- **Technical SEO** is about making websites faster, mobile-friendly, error-free, and easy to find.
- Common issues include site speed, mobile-friendliness, broken links, XML sitemaps, and robots.txt files.
- **Pro Tip** 💡: Fix these issues regularly to keep your site in top shape for users and search engines alike!

SEO Joke to Finish:
Why do websites love SEO?
Because it helps them make *new friends* on the internet! 😄

Lesson 2: Site Speed Optimization

Introduction: Why Does Site Speed Matter for SEO? 🚀
Imagine you're excited to play a video game, but it takes forever to load. Would you wait, or would you move on to something else? Well, websites are the same way.

When people click on a website and it loads too slowly, they usually don't wait. Instead, they move on to another website. This can make the website owner lose visitors, and search engines, like Google, notice that!

In this lesson, we'll learn why site speed is super important for SEO, and I'll share easy ways to speed up any website.

How Site Speed Impacts SEO □

1. Visitor Happiness ☺
When a site loads fast, visitors are happy, and they're more likely to stay and explore. If it's slow, they leave! Google, Bing, and other search engines notice this because they want to show search results that make people happy.

If visitors keep leaving a slow website, search engines think it must not be a good website to show first.

Example: Imagine if you were looking for "best cookie recipes." You find a website, but it's so slow that it feels like *forever* before you see the recipe. You might click back and choose a faster site. Google sees that lots of people are leaving, so it ranks that slow site lower.

2. Ranking Boosts! 📈

Fast websites usually rank higher because search engines consider speed when deciding which sites are the best. Faster sites often get a "thumbs up" from Google, which means better rankings. So, if you're working on SEO, making a site faster is a smart move!

> 😄 **SEO Joke:** Why did the slow website break up with its visitors? Because they just couldn't wait for each other!

Techniques to Improve Load Time ⚡

Alright, let's dive into some easy (and fun!) ways to make websites faster. Each technique can make a difference, especially when used together.

And yes, even the smallest tweaks can have a big impact on site speed!

1. Image Compression □

Images are often the "biggest" thing on a website and can take a long time to load. Compressing images means making the file sizes smaller without making the pictures look fuzzy. This way, the website loads much faster.

- **How to Do It:** You can use tools like **TinyPNG** or **ImageOptim** to shrink images.
- **Example:** Suppose you have a website with a lot of photos of adorable puppies. If each photo is 2MB, that's a lot for the page to load! Compressing those images to 500KB each can make the page load four times faster.

  Pro Tip: Use the right image format! For photos, **JPEG** is usually best; for logos and icons, **PNG** or **SVG** works well.

2. Browser Caching 💼

Caching is like asking a visitor's browser (like Chrome or Safari) to remember certain parts of a website. So, when they visit again, the browser doesn't have to load everything from scratch. Instead, it just "remembers" and loads faster.

- **How to Do It:** Many platforms, like WordPress, have caching plugins like **W3 Total Cache** or **WP Super Cache** to make this easy.
- **Example:** Think of caching like having all your favorite toys already laid out on the table. You don't have to dig through a toy box every time you want to play, and it's much quicker!

😄 **SEO Joke:** Why did the website get so many repeat visitors? Because they knew it had a "cache" of fun! 💰

---

3. Minify JavaScript, CSS, and HTML 🗜️

JavaScript, CSS, and HTML are the "languages" that websites use to look good and work well. But sometimes they have a lot of extra spaces, comments, and codes that don't actually help the website look any different. Minifying means taking out those extras to make the code smaller and faster to load.

- **How to Do It:** Tools like **Minify Code** or plugins like **Autoptimize** can handle this.
- **Example:** Imagine you're writing a long story but only want to share the important parts. Minifying is like cutting out the "fluff" so readers get straight to the story.

  💡 **Pro Tip:** Many website builders like Squarespace or Wix handle minification automatically, so you don't have to worry about this if you're using them.

---

4. Use a Content Delivery Network (CDN) ☐

A CDN is a network of servers around the world. Instead of loading your website from one place, a CDN lets people load it from a server close to them, which makes it load faster.

- **How to Do It:** Services like **Cloudflare** and **Amazon CloudFront** offer CDN services.

- **Example:** Think of it like a pizza delivery. If the pizza shop is next door, the pizza gets to you faster. CDNs make sure your website "delivers" from the nearest location to the visitor.

😄 **SEO Joke:** Why did the website start using a CDN? Because it wanted to be closer to its users… and serve them *super* fast!

---

5. Reduce Redirects ☐

Redirects are like detours. When there are too many of them, it takes visitors longer to reach the content they want. Fewer redirects = faster load times!

- **How to Do It:** Go through the website and remove any redirects that aren't necessary.
- **Example:** Imagine you're trying to go to a friend's house, but you keep taking wrong turns. Fewer detours mean you'll get there faster, just like a website page.

♀ Pro Tip: Avoid linking to old pages if you can. Update links to the latest pages so that visitors (and Google) don't have to take extra steps to find your content.

---

6. Use Faster Hosting 💻

Web hosting is like the home for your website. If the host is slow, it can slow down the whole website. Choosing a good host can make a big difference in speed.

- **How to Do It:** Research hosting providers like **SiteGround**, **Bluehost**, or **A2 Hosting**, which are known for fast loading times.
- **Example:** Imagine you're at a library, and it takes forever for the librarian to find your book. A better library (or host) makes everything quicker!

♀ Pro Tip: Go for a host that offers SSD (Solid State Drives) storage, which loads faster than traditional storage.

Wrapping Up: Keep It Fast and Keep It Fun!

By making a website faster, you're not only making visitors happy, but you're also helping it rank higher on Google. Remember, search engines want to show the best results, and a fast website is always a good result!

Quick Summary:

- **Image Compression** helps pages load quicker without losing quality.
- **Browser Caching** allows return visitors to load pages faster.
- **Minifying Code** cuts out unnecessary bits to make code smaller.
- **CDNs** bring content closer to the user.
- **Fewer Redirects** mean fewer detours.
- **Faster Hosting** gives the website a solid "home base."

  😊 **Final SEO Joke:** Why did the website go to a speed boot camp? Because it was

tired of being left behind in the rankings!
🏃

By using these tips, you'll have a website that's fast, friendly, and loved by both visitors and search engines. Happy optimizing! 🎈

Lesson 3: Mobile Friendliness and Responsive Design

Welcome to Lesson 3 of our SEO e-book! Let's talk about mobile-friendliness and responsive design and why these are super important for websites today.

Imagine trying to read a book that's too big for your hands – annoying, right? Now, think about how people feel when they visit a website that doesn't fit nicely on their phone screen. That's where mobile-friendliness comes in! Ready to learn? Let's dive in! 😊

Importance of Mobile Optimization in SEO

What is Mobile Optimization?

Mobile optimization is making sure a website looks good and works well on phones, tablets, and other smaller devices. It's like magic that makes the website "fit" the screen, so it's easy to see, read, and click on things without zooming in or getting frustrated.

Why Does Mobile Optimization Matter?

1. **More People Use Mobile Devices:** Over **60% of web searches are done on mobile devices** – that's like most of the people in a candy store choosing gummy bears over chocolates!

2. **Google Cares About Mobile Optimization:** Google uses a "mobile-first index," which means it checks how a website works on mobile before ranking it in search results. If a site works well on mobile, Google gives it a thumbs up 👍, which can help it rank higher.

3. **Better User Experience:** When people visit a mobile-friendly site, they're happier, stay longer, and are more likely to visit again. And Google loves happy visitors!

4. **Faster Loading Speed:** Mobile-friendly sites are usually faster because they load only what's needed, making users feel like they're browsing at lightning speed!

   SEO Joke Alert!
   Why did the website break up with mobile optimization?
   It couldn't keep up with the speed!

Example

Imagine you're on a website on your phone, and you need to keep zooming in and out to read the text. Frustrating, right? Now picture a mobile-friendly site where everything is neatly arranged to fit your screen perfectly – no zooming needed! Which one would you stay on longer? Probably the second one, right? That's why mobile-friendliness is key!

Pro Tip 💡

Always test your website on different devices to make sure it looks good on each one. A site that works well on both a phone and a computer is like a superhero with more than one power!

Guidelines for Mobile-First Design and UX

1. Responsive Design: Adapting to All Screen Sizes

Responsive design means the website can adjust its layout based on the screen size it's being viewed on. It's like a magical rubber band that stretches and shrinks to fit any device – from tiny phones to big computers.

- **Example:** Think of a responsive website like a piece of clay. You can mold it into any shape to fit any space without losing its main design.
- **Data Fact: 91% of mobile users say access to content is very important**. If the content is squished or out of place, they'll leave!

2. Use Bigger, Touchable Buttons

On mobile, you tap instead of click. So, buttons need to be big enough for fingers! Small buttons can make users accidentally click the wrong thing, which can be annoying.

- **Example:** Imagine a game with tiny controls versus one with big, easy-to-tap buttons. Which one would you prefer on a phone?
- **Pro Tip 💡:** *Make buttons at least 48x48 pixels – it's like giving fingers a nice, big target!*

3. Simple and Clear Navigation

Mobile screens are smaller, so keep navigation menus simple and easy to understand. When someone visits a site, they shouldn't feel lost. Just like a treasure map, directions should be clear so people can find what they're looking for.

- **Example:** A desktop site might have a big menu with ten options, but on mobile, the menu is hidden in a small "hamburger" icon (three horizontal lines) that opens up when tapped.
- **SEO Joke Alert!** 😂
  Why did the mobile site get lost?
  It didn't follow the navigation!

4. Optimize Images for Faster Loading

Big images can make a site load slowly on mobile, which is like waiting for paint to dry! Optimizing images means shrinking them without losing quality so the page loads faster.

- **Example:** If an image on your website is like a giant poster, you can resize it to a smaller photo size for mobile users. This makes loading faster and smoother.
- **Data Fact:** A delay of just **3 seconds** can make **53% of mobile users leave** a page. Keeping images small and loading fast is a big deal!

5. Minimize Pop-Ups on Mobile

Pop-ups are those little boxes that show up on top of content, asking you to subscribe or check out an offer. On mobile, pop-ups can be annoying if they're too big and cover up everything else.

- **Example:** A small pop-up that only takes up a small portion of the screen is okay, but a huge one can make people feel like they're stuck in a maze with no exit.

- **Pro Tip 💡:** *Use pop-ups only when necessary on mobile and make them easy to close!*

6. Readable Fonts for All Screens

Choose fonts that are easy to read on small screens. If the font is too tiny, users may have to squint, which can be uncomfortable.

- **Example:** Think of it like writing on a sticky note versus a full-sized paper. You'd want your handwriting bigger on the sticky note so it's easy to read, right? Same with mobile fonts – keep them big enough to read without squinting!
- **SEO Joke Alert!** 😊
  Why don't SEO experts use small fonts? They don't want their visitors squinting and bouncing away!

Mobile-First Design: The Google-Favored Approach

Google's mobile-first approach means it looks at how the mobile version of your website works when deciding its ranking. So, if your site is ready for mobile, it's ready for Google!

- **Data Fact: 80% of top-ranked websites** are optimized for mobile. When you optimize for mobile, you're telling Google, "I'm ready to be at the top!" 👑

How to Approach Mobile-First Design

1. **Start Small, Then Go Big:** Design for the smallest screen first (like a phone) and then adapt for bigger screens. It's easier to add things for larger screens than to make things smaller for a mobile screen.
2. **Prioritize Content**: Only put the most important content on mobile. Nobody likes clutter, especially on a small screen!
   - **Example:** If you were writing a story, you'd keep only the important parts in a summary. In mobile design, do the same – only show what users really need!

Pro Tip 💡

Before launching, try visiting your website on different devices – iPhones, Android phones, tablets – to see how it looks and feels. Testing is the secret ingredient to a perfect mobile design!

Summary

Mobile-friendliness and responsive design are like the keys to a smooth user experience and higher rankings on Google. When your website looks and works great on a phone, Google (and visitors) will be happy! With guidelines like using readable fonts, having clear navigation, and making your site fast and simple, you'll be on the right path to mobile success. So remember – a happy mobile site makes for a happy Google ranking! 😊

Lesson 4: Crawlability and Indexing

Welcome to another fun part of SEO! Here, we'll dive into how search engines like Google find and save content from the web.

Think of it like a treasure hunt where search engines look for clues (your content!) and store it to show people later. Plus, I've thrown in some jokes and pro tips to make this adventure even cooler. Let's go! 🕵️‍♂️

---

1. How Search Engines Crawl and Index Content

Imagine a little robot called a "crawler" visiting websites. It's like a curious bug that goes around looking at all the pages on the internet. These crawlers don't just look; they also "read" the pages and take notes.

Once a crawler reads a page, it's ready for the next step—**indexing**. In indexing, the information is saved in a giant library (or database). So when someone searches for something, like "How to bake cookies," Google knows which pages to show that have cookie recipes.

Example: If you have a website about toys, a crawler might visit your site, read about all your toys, and save that info. Now, when someone searches "fun toys for kids," your page might appear!

SEO Joke 😄: Why did the search engine crawler break up with the website? It just didn't have the *right keywords*!

Pro Tip 💡: Make it easy for crawlers by having a simple layout and linking to important pages from your homepage. Think of it as giving the crawler a map of your site!

---

2. Why Crawlability and Indexing Matter

Crawlability and indexing are super important because they help search engines find your pages. Without these, your pages would be like secret rooms that nobody can enter. Making sure your pages are crawlable and indexed helps your site get more visitors!

When your site is crawlable, it's like saying, "Hey, Google! Come check out my stuff!" And when it's indexed, it's like being added to Google's big "book of cool things." This way, people can discover your page easily.

Example: Let's say you make a blog post called "Top 10 Board Games." If it's not indexed, it's hidden from search engines, so no one will find it in search results. But if it's indexed, people looking for board games can read your post!

SEO Joke 😂: Why did the crawler need a nap? It had a *page-load* of work!

Pro Tip 💡: Use Google Search Console (it's free!) to check if your pages are indexed and to see if Google has found any crawl issues.

3. Fixing Crawl Errors

Sometimes, crawlers run into obstacles—like a locked door or a dead-end road. These obstacles are called "crawl errors," and they make it hard for search engines to reach your content.

There are two main types of crawl errors:

1. **Site Errors**: These mean the entire website has a problem.
2. **Page Errors**: These mean only specific pages have an issue, like when a page doesn't load properly.

Example: A common page error is called a "404 error." This happens when a page is missing. Imagine a crawler clicking a link that says, "Awesome Toy Cars," but when it gets there, it finds nothing. That's a 404 error!

How to Fix Crawl Errors:

*   **Redirect**: If you delete a page, set up a redirect to a similar page.

- **Fix Links**: Check for broken links and fix or remove them.
- **Clear Blockers**: Make sure your pages aren't accidentally "locked" by special codes like robots.txt, which tells crawlers to avoid certain pages.

SEO Joke 😊: What did the crawler say to the 404 error page? "I guess I'll *skip* this one!"

Pro Tip 💡: Use Google Search Console to see any crawl errors and how to fix them!

---

4. Improving Indexability

Once a crawler finds your page, the next step is to help it get stored (or "indexed") so it appears in search results. Here's how you can make your pages easier for search engines to index:

- **Optimize Your Titles and Headings**: Titles (like "Top Toy Picks for Kids") tell Google what the page is about.

- **Use Descriptive URLs**: URLs like "mytoystore.com/best-cars" are better than "mytoystore.com/p=123."
- **Create a Sitemap**: A sitemap is like a treasure map for crawlers. It lists all the pages you want them to find and makes crawling super easy.

Example: If you have a "Contact Us" page, having a descriptive URL like "mytoystore.com/contact-us" helps search engines know it's where people can find your contact info.

SEO Joke 😄: How do crawlers and librarians work together? They both love *indexing* things!

Pro Tip 💡: You can create a sitemap using tools like Yoast SEO (for WordPress users) or online sitemap generators. After that, submit it in Google Search Console so crawlers know exactly where to go.

---

5. Checking Crawlability and Indexing with Google Search Console

Google Search Console is like a report card for your website. It helps you see how Google is crawling and indexing your pages. Here's how to use it:

1. **Check Coverage**: Go to the "Coverage" section to see which pages are indexed and which have errors.
2. **Fix Errors**: You'll get a list of pages with problems. Google even tells you how to fix them!
3. **Request Indexing**: If you create a new page, you can request Google to index it. It's like saying, "Hey, Google! I've got something new for you!"

Example: If you write a new blog post called "Top 10 Fun Games for Kids," you can ask Google Search Console to index it right away. This makes it appear in search results faster!

SEO Joke 😄: Why did the SEO expert start a garden? Because they heard crawlers love fresh content!

Pro Tip 💡: Check Google Search Console monthly to make sure your site is healthy and error-free.

Summary

In SEO, getting crawlers to find and index your site is like opening the doors to new visitors. It's a way of saying, "Come in and take a look!" By fixing crawl errors and improving indexability, your pages become easier to find. And remember, tools like Google Search Console are there to help you make this journey even smoother!

Quick Recap:

- **Crawling**: Crawlers find and read your pages.
- **Indexing**: Search engines save your page info to show people later.
- **Fix Errors**: Use Google Search Console to catch and fix crawl issues.
- **Be Index-Ready**: Optimize titles, URLs, and sitemaps to boost indexability.

SEO Joke 😄: Why was the SEO book so calm? Because it was all about *index*ed content!

Happy Crawling and Indexing!

Lesson 5: Sitemaps and Robots.txt Files

Welcome to our lesson on sitemaps and robots.txt files! Imagine these two tools as a treasure map and a security guard for a website. They help search engines like Google and Bing know where to find the good stuff on your website and where *not* to go. Here's how they work in the SEO world!

What is a Sitemap?

Think of a sitemap as a "website map" that shows search engines all the pages on your website. It's like giving them a list of everything you want them to find so they don't miss anything important.

Why Sitemaps Matter in SEO

Sitemaps are especially important for SEO because they make sure search engines know about every page on your site. If you have new pages or updates, a sitemap tells Google, "Hey, I have new stuff here!"

Without a sitemap, search engines might skip some pages.

> **Example:** Let's say you have a website about animal facts. Your sitemap would list all the animal pages like "Lions," "Penguins," and "Elephants" so that search engines can find every single one.

😄 **SEO Joke:** Why did the search engine bring a map to the website? Because it didn't want to get "lost in translation!"

💡 **Pro Tip:** If you add a new page, update your sitemap so search engines notice it faster.

How to Create a Sitemap

There are different ways to create a sitemap, but using tools can make it easy!

1. **Use a Sitemap Generator Tool:** Tools like **XML Sitemap Generator** or **Screaming Frog** can automatically create a sitemap for you.

2. **Save as XML Format:** Sitemaps are usually saved in XML format, which looks like a code language but is easy for search engines to read.
3. **Upload the Sitemap to Your Website:** Place the sitemap file in your website's root folder. For example, it might look like:

   `www.mywebsite.com/sitemap.xml`.

   Example: If you're using WordPress, plugins like **Yoast SEO** can automatically create and update your sitemap whenever you add or edit pages.

💡 **Pro Tip:** Make sure to submit your sitemap to Google Search Console so that Google always has the latest version!

What is a Robots.txt File?

Now, the robots.txt file is like a security guard for your website. It tells search engines where they can or can't go.

Why Robots.txt Files Matter in SEO

This file can help keep certain parts of your website private. For example, you might want to stop search engines from crawling pages that are under construction or personal pages.

> **Example:** Imagine you have a "Thank You" page that appears after someone signs up for your email list. You might not want search engines to show this page in search results, so you can tell them not to look at it using robots.txt.

☺ **SEO Joke:** Why did the robot stay out of the website? Because robots.txt told it, "No entry!"

How to Create a Robots.txt File

Creating a robots.txt file is easy! It's just a text file that lists some simple instructions for search engines. Here's how:

1. **Open a Text Editor:** Use Notepad or TextEdit to create the file.
2. **Add Instructions for Crawlers:** Use basic commands like `Disallow` to block certain pages and `Allow` to allow others.
3. **Upload to Root Folder:** Save the file as `robots.txt` and place it in the main folder of your website.

Example: A simple robots.txt file might look like this:

plaintext
Copy code
```
User-agent: *
Disallow: /private/
Allow: /public/
```

Here's what this means:

- **User-agent:** * = It applies to all search engines.
- **Disallow:** /private/ = Search engines won't look at any page in the "private" folder.
- **Allow:** /public/ = Search engines can look at the "public" folder.

💡 Pro Tip: Test your robots.txt file using Google Search Console's "Robots Testing Tool" to make sure it's blocking or allowing the right pages.

Optimizing Your Sitemap and Robots.txt Files

Optimizing Your Sitemap

1. **Keep Your Sitemap Updated:** Make sure it includes all current pages but removes any that don't exist anymore.
2. **Include Important Pages Only:** Only add pages that you want search engines to find; don't include "unimportant" pages like thank-you or test pages.
3. **Set Priority Levels:** Some sitemap tools allow you to set priority levels for pages. For example, your homepage might be higher priority than a blog post.

   Example: If you're running a blog, you'll want to prioritize your main categories or

popular posts, like "Best Animal Facts,"
over less critical ones.

Optimizing Your Robots.txt

1. **Block Duplicate Content:** If you have pages
   with similar content (like printable pages), you
   can tell search engines to ignore them.
2. **Protect Private Information:** If there are parts
   of your website you don't want anyone to see,
   robots.txt can help.
3. **Avoid Blocking Essential Files:** Don't
   accidentally block CSS or JavaScript files
   because they help search engines understand
   your website better.

   Example: Let's say you run an online
   store with customer info. Use robots.txt to
   keep any sensitive pages hidden.

☺ **SEO Joke:** Why don't robots.txt and sitemaps get
along? Because one says "Come in!" and the other
says "Stay out!"

Pro Tip: Review your robots.txt file regularly to make sure it's not accidentally blocking any pages you want search engines to crawl.

Submitting Sitemaps and Robots.txt Files to Search Engines

After you've created and optimized your files, you want to make sure search engines see them.

How to Submit Your Sitemap

1. **Google Search Console:** Go to Google Search Console and find "Sitemaps." Enter the URL for your sitemap, and hit "Submit."
2. **Bing Webmaster Tools:** Bing has a similar tool. Just add your sitemap URL, and Bing will crawl it.

   Example: If your sitemap URL is `www.mywebsite.com/sitemap.xml`, that's what you'll submit.

How to Check Your Robots.txt File

1. **Google Search Console's Robots Testing Tool:** Paste your robots.txt file's URL, and Google will show you if there are any problems.
2. **Bing Webmaster Tools:** Bing also has a robots.txt tester.

😄 **SEO Joke:** Why did the sitemap break up with robots.txt? Because they didn't "crawl" in the same direction!

Summary

- **Sitemap:** Shows search engines the pages you want them to find. Keep it updated and submit it to Google and Bing for best results.
- **Robots.txt:** Controls where search engines can go on your website. Use it to block private or duplicate pages.
- **Optimization Tips:** Regularly review and update both files to ensure they're helping your SEO goals.

With these tools in place, your website will be easy for search engines to navigate, while protecting sensitive pages from being found. Sitemaps lead search engines to the best parts of your website, and robots.txt helps guard areas you'd rather keep private. Together, they're a perfect SEO team!

Lesson 6: Structured Data and Schema Markup

What is Schema Markup, and How Does It Help SEO?

Imagine you have a big treasure chest filled with toys, but it's all mixed up. If your mom wanted to find your favorite stuffed animal, she'd have to search through everything. Now, imagine if you labeled all your toys with tags that say, "stuffed animal," "puzzle," or "building blocks." Your mom would find things quickly!

That's kind of what schema markup does for websites. It's a way of organizing information so that search engines like Google can "see" what's on the page more clearly. With schema markup, search engines can understand if you're sharing a recipe, a review, or a movie, which helps make the information appear in richer, more exciting ways on search pages.

SEO Joke:
Why did the schema markup go to school?
To get a little "structured" education! 😂

Section 1: What is Schema Markup?

Schema markup is code you add to your website that "labels" your content for search engines. This special code helps search engines understand exactly what your page is about, making it easier for them to show your website in cool formats, like star ratings for reviews, event dates, or recipe images!

For example, let's say you run a bakery and have a website with cupcake recipes. With schema markup, you can label parts of your recipe page, like the ingredients, cook time, and star ratings. Google can then show your recipe with these labels in search results. This extra info, called "rich snippets," makes people more likely to click your link!

Example:
Without schema: *"Cupcake recipe"*
With schema: *"Cupcake recipe (includes 4.5-star rating, 20-minute bake time, 5 ingredients)"*

Pro Tip 💡 **:** *Using schema markup can increase your click-through rate by up to 30%! This is because people love clicking on links with more information right in the search results.*

Section 2: Why Does Schema Markup Matter for SEO?

Schema markup gives your website a better chance to show up in "rich results." Rich results are search results with extra details, like images, ratings, or even videos. These types of results grab people's attention and make your site look more helpful and professional.

When your website shows up with these extra details, it usually gets more clicks because it looks more inviting and informative. More clicks can mean more traffic, which is great for SEO because search engines like Google notice when people are interested in your site.

Example:
A normal search result looks like this:
"Bakery in New York - Delicious cupcakes and pastries"

With schema markup, it could look like this:
"Bakery in New York - ⋆ 4.8 - Known for Red Velvet Cupcakes - Open today until 8 PM"

SEO Joke:
What did the schema say to the website?
"You complete me!" 😄

Section 3: Types of Schema Markup You Can Use

There are many types of schema markup you can use, depending on your content. Here are a few popular ones that help websites stand out in search results:

1. **Recipe Schema** – For food bloggers or recipe sites, this markup highlights ingredients, cooking time, and even calories.
2. **Review Schema** – This one's useful for adding star ratings, which can show up under your site link in search results, making it look more credible.
3. **Event Schema** – Use this if you're hosting events; it lets people see the event's date, location, and even price if they search for it.
4. **Product Schema** – Great for e-commerce! It shows details like price, stock level, and reviews.

Example:
If you own a bookstore and use product schema, your search result could show something like this:
"*Harry Potter Book – *4.9 rating – $15 – In stock*"

Pro Tip 💡: *If you want your pages to appear in rich results, start with the schema that matches your main* *content. Adding recipe schema to a blog post might not be as useful as adding it to an actual recipe.*

Section 4: How to Implement Schema Markup

Now, you might be wondering, "How do I get this special schema code onto my website?" Here's a simple way to get started:

1. **Use Google's Structured Data Markup Helper**: Google has a tool that makes it easy. You just paste your page's URL, select the data type (like "Recipe" or "Event"), and then highlight the information on the page. Google will help you create the code you need!

2. **Add the Code to Your Website**: After creating the code, you copy it and add it to your website's HTML. If you're not familiar with coding, you might need a little help from someone who knows. Or, if your website uses

a platform like WordPress, there are plugins that can help you add schema without any coding.

3. **Test It Out**: Google also has a testing tool called the Structured Data Testing Tool. You can paste your page URL to see if Google detects the schema correctly.

SEO Joke:
Why did the schema markup break up with the HTML?
Because it found something more structured! 😄

Example of Code:
Here's a snippet of schema code for a cupcake recipe:

html
Copy code
```
<script type="application/ld+json">
{
  "@context": "http://schema.org",
  "@type": "Recipe",
  "name": "Chocolate Cupcake",
  "cookTime": "PT20M",
```

```
  "recipeIngredient": [
    "1 cup flour",
    "1/2 cup sugar",
    "1/4 cup cocoa powder",
    "1/2 cup butter"
  ],
  "recipeInstructions": "Mix all
ingredients and bake at 350°F for 20
minutes."
}
</script>
```

Pro Tip 💡: *Schema markup is like sprinkles on a cupcake—small but makes it way more appealing! Add schema in a way that truly highlights the most valuable parts of your page.*

Section 5: Testing and Validating Your Schema Markup

Once you've added schema markup, it's a good idea to make sure it's working correctly. Testing helps ensure Google will recognize your schema and show it properly.

Testing Tools:

1. **Google Rich Results Test**: Check if your schema can generate rich results.
2. **Schema.org Validator**: Another tool that tests if your schema is correctly formatted.

Testing is important because if there are errors, Google might ignore your markup, and you won't get rich results. Just like a recipe, if you forget an ingredient, the outcome might not be what you expect!

Example:
Imagine you run the Rich Results Test on your cupcake recipe page. If there are errors, it might say something like "missing cook time." Fixing this will ensure Google can read it correctly.

Section 6: How Schema Markup Benefits You (and Searchers)

By using schema markup, you're making things easier not only for Google but also for people searching online. This improved understanding of your site can lead to:

- **Higher Click-Through Rates**: Rich results attract more eyes!
- **Increased Trust**: People trust sites that show rich, detailed snippets in search.
- **More Conversions**: For businesses, detailed info in search results often means more customers!

SEO Joke:
Why did the structured data win the "Best Website" award?
Because it was organized to the core! 😄

Conclusion: Schema Markup is SEO's Secret Ingredient!
Adding schema markup is like adding magic labels to

your website content. These labels help search engines understand what's on your page and show it in fun, interesting ways.

Pro Tip 💡 : *Don't worry if you can't add schema to every page. Start with your top pages, like product pages or your main blog posts, to see the best results.*

With schema, you can give search engines—and your users—a better experience, just like a well-organized toy chest makes playtime more fun and easy!

Lesson 7: Canonicalization and URL Structure

1. Why Canonicalization Matters

Imagine you have two identical superhero action figures. If you put both on display, people might get confused about which one is the "real" star of the show! Search engines feel the same way when they find duplicate content (like two web pages with the same info).

Canonicalization is like putting a little label on the "main" action figure saying, "This is the original!" So, it tells search engines which page to rank for that content.

Example:
Say you have two pages that look exactly alike:

- `https://example.com/dentist-services`
- `https://example.com/services/dentist-services`

To avoid confusing search engines, you can add a canonical tag to tell Google which one is the real hero!

SEO Joke:
😄 *Why did the duplicate page go to therapy? Because it had an identity crisis!*

Pro Tip 💡
Always set a canonical tag for pages with similar content to avoid confusion with search engines. It helps your "main" page stay in the spotlight!

2. Avoiding Duplicate Content with Canonical Tags

Duplicate content is like repeating the same joke twice—it doesn't land as well the second time! For websites, having duplicate content means search engines don't know which page to show users, which could lower your site's ranking.

Canonical tags solve this by pointing out the *one* page that should rank.

How Canonical Tags Work

Adding a canonical tag is like saying, "This is the main page!" It's done in the HTML of a webpage like this:

html
Copy code
```
<link rel="canonical"
href="https://example.com/main-page">
```

Example:
If you have a product page that can be accessed through different paths, like:

- `https://example.com/shoes`
- `https://example.com/all-products/shoes`

Then, you'd add a canonical tag on one of them to point to the main page.

Fun Fact:
40% of SEO experts say that avoiding duplicate content with canonical tags has helped improve their site rankings!

Pro Tip 💡
When making a new page with similar content, always add a canonical tag on the page you want to rank higher. This helps search engines focus on the main content without spreading ranking power thinly across duplicates.

---

3. Best Practices for Canonicalization

For your website to work smoothly with search engines, here's a quick guide:

- **Keep it Simple:** Always point the canonical tag to the URL you want to rank.
- **Check URLs Regularly:** Make sure canonical tags don't point to pages that are broken or deleted.
- **Only Use One Canonical Tag per Page:** Just like one title for a movie, every page should have only one canonical URL.

SEO Joke:

😄 *How many canonical tags does it take to fix a duplicate content issue? Just one—more than that, and even Google gets confused!*

Example:

Let's say you have multiple URLs for the same blog post. Use a canonical tag on each duplicate page that points to the main URL. For instance:

- Main page URL:
  ```
  https://example.com/blog/best-
  trekking-tips
  ```
- Duplicate URL:
  ```
  https://example.com/blog/trekking-
  tips-best
  ```

Add a canonical tag to the duplicate page
pointing to the main URL.

Pro Tip 💡
If you're using a CMS like WordPress, many plugins
can automatically add canonical tags for you. Check
them out to make your job easier!

---

4. Creating SEO-Friendly URLs

An SEO-friendly URL is like a clean and simple road
sign for search engines and users. It should be easy to
read, understand, and remember.

Best Practices for URLs:

1. **Keep It Short and Sweet:** A URL should
   ideally be 3-5 words long. Long URLs can
   confuse people and search engines.
2. **Use Hyphens, Not Underscores:** Hyphens (-)
   between words make URLs more readable.
3. **Include Your Main Keyword:** If your page is
   about "dog training," try using it in the URL, like
   `https://example.com/dog-training`.

Example:

If you're making a page about dental services, use `https://example.com/dental-services` instead of `https://example.com/our-amazing-top-quality-dental-services-for-you`.

SEO Joke:

😄 *Why did the long URL break up with the search engine? It just had too much baggage!*

Pro Tip 💡

To improve readability, avoid using unnecessary words like "and," "the," or numbers that don't add value. Short and sweet URLs are easy for both search engines and humans to understand!

---

5. Using Keywords in URLs: Does It Help?

Keywords in URLs can give a little boost to your SEO, but don't overdo it! It's like putting a cherry on top— nice, but not necessary for the whole cake.

Examples of Good and Not-So-Good URLs:

- **Good URL:** `https://example.com/kids-dentist-tips`
- **Not-So-Good URL:** `https://example.com/5y9d-tips-and-tricks-for-kids-dentist-jks9274`

Fun Fact:
About 15% of top-ranking pages use simple, keyword-focused URLs.

Pro Tip 💡
When In doubt, make your URL as natural and readable as possible. If it looks complicated, try simplifying it by removing extra words or irrelevant numbers.

---

6. Avoiding URL Mistakes

Even SEO superheroes can make mistakes with URLs. Here are some common ones to avoid:

- **Using Dynamic Parameters Too Much:** URLs with symbols like "?" and "&" are harder to read.

- **Ignoring Capitalization:** URLs should be all lowercase. Capitals might create duplicates, which we want to avoid.
- **Skipping Redirects:** If you change a URL, always set up a redirect to send visitors to the new page, or else it's like closing a door without putting up a sign.

Example:

Instead of `https://example.com/Best-Products?Version=1234`, try `https://example.com/best-products`.

SEO Joke:

😄 *Why did the URL refuse to go on vacation? Because it didn't want to get redirected!*

Pro Tip 💡

Always double-check your URLs when creating new pages or moving old ones. Redirects ensure that visitors and search engines end up in the right place without getting lost.

Wrapping Up: Canonicalization and URL Structure

Canonicalization and URL structure might sound tricky, but with a few simple rules, you can make sure search engines see the right pages and your URLs stay user-friendly. Remember:

- **Canonical tags** are your friends when you have duplicate content. Use them wisely.
- **SEO-friendly URLs** are short, readable, and contain keywords.
- Avoid common mistakes with URLs to keep your site easy to navigate.

Final SEO Joke:
☺ *Why did the SEO specialist bring a ladder to the website? Because they wanted to reach the top of the rankings!*

With these tips, you're all set to create a strong foundation for your website's SEO through proper canonicalization and clear URL structure! Happy optimizing!

Lesson 8: HTTP vs. HTTPS – SSL and Site Security

1. What is HTTP vs. HTTPS?

HTTP stands for **HyperText Transfer Protocol**. This is the basic language that web browsers (like Chrome or Safari) and websites use to talk to each other. But with HTTP, the messages are like a postcard: everyone who handles it on the way can read it! 😵

HTTPS is like the "secure" version of HTTP. It stands for **HyperText Transfer Protocol Secure**. HTTPS makes sure that nobody can "eavesdrop" on your messages by adding a **security layer** called **SSL (Secure Sockets Layer)**. So, it's like sending a letter in a sealed envelope that only the recipient can open! ▢ 🔒

SEO Joke: Why did the website bring an umbrella? Because it switched to HTTPS for safer surfing! 😄

---

2. Why is HTTPS Important for SEO?

Google loves websites that are safe and trustworthy. It's like preferring a well-lit park over a dark alley. If your website has HTTPS, Google feels safer recommending it to people, so it's more likely to appear higher in search results!

Some important reasons HTTPS helps SEO include:

- **Trust**: Visitors trust HTTPS sites more, and they are less likely to leave right away.
- **Google Ranking Boost**: Since 2014, Google has used HTTPS as a "ranking signal." It's like a mini boost in the race to the top of search results.

Example: Imagine you have two websites: "SunnyBooks.com" (HTTP) and "SunnyBooks.com" (HTTPS). If everything else is the same, Google will probably rank the HTTPS version higher!

Pro Tip 💡: To check if a website is HTTPS, look for the little lock 🔒 symbol in the URL bar.

---

3. How HTTPS Protects Visitors

HTTPS uses **SSL certificates** to encrypt data. This means if someone tries to peek, all they'll see is scrambled letters and numbers instead of your sensitive info.

Here's how it works:

1. **Browser checks SSL certificate**: When you visit an HTTPS site, your browser checks for the site's SSL certificate to make sure it's secure.
2. **Data encryption**: Once approved, all data (like passwords or payment info) is sent in a coded language that only the website can decode.

Example: Think of sending a message like "Hello." With HTTPS, it becomes something like "H7!K#oX." Only the website's special code can turn "H7!K#oX" back into "Hello." ☺

SEO Joke: Why did the hacker break up with the HTTP site? Because it just wasn't secure! ☺

---

4. Steps to Implement SSL on Your Site

Adding SSL to your site isn't as hard as it sounds! Here are the basic steps:

1. **Choose an SSL Certificate Provider**: These can be free (like Let's Encrypt) or paid (like Comodo or GoDaddy).
2. **Install the SSL Certificate on Your Server**: Most web hosts, like Bluehost or SiteGround, offer easy installation guides or even automatic setups.
3. **Update URLs to HTTPS**: After SSL is installed, you'll need to change your website's URLs from HTTP to HTTPS.
4. **Redirect Old Links**: Any links to your old HTTP pages should be redirected to the HTTPS versions so visitors don't end up on an unsecured page.

Pro Tip 💡: Some hosting providers include SSL certificates for free with their hosting plans, so look out for these deals to save money!

---

5. Benefits of HTTPS Beyond SEO

HTTPS isn't just good for SEO; it also helps your users and your business in other ways:

- **Increases Visitor Trust**: People feel safer on HTTPS sites, which keeps them on your site longer.
- **Protects Against Hackers**: HTTPS prevents hackers from intercepting data, which is crucial for websites handling sensitive information.

Example: Imagine visiting a bank website. Would you feel safe if you saw "Not Secure" in the URL bar? Probably not! With HTTPS, you get that little lock symbol, so you know it's safe to use.

SEO Joke: What did the HTTP website say to the HTTPS website? "I can't handle the *security* of this relationship!" 😄

---

6. Common Myths about HTTPS

Sometimes people think HTTPS isn't necessary if they don't sell things or collect data, but that's a myth! HTTPS makes your website faster and more secure, and Google loves secure sites. Here's the truth:

- **Myth**: "I don't collect info, so I don't need HTTPS."
  Fact: Even basic sites benefit from HTTPS. Google ranks HTTPS sites higher, and visitors are more likely to trust them.
- **Myth**: "HTTPS makes my site slower."
  Fact: HTTPS can actually speed up your site. With HTTPS, you can enable faster browsing features like HTTP/2.

Pro Tip 💡: Check out free SSL certificate options like Let's Encrypt if you want a cost-effective solution.

---

7. How HTTPS Impacts SEO Metrics

Switching to HTTPS can improve important SEO metrics that affect your ranking:

- **Lower Bounce Rate**: Visitors feel more secure, so they're less likely to leave immediately.
- **Better Conversion Rates**: A secure site is crucial for e-commerce. HTTPS boosts trust, so

people are more likely to make purchases or sign up.

Example Data: According to studies, over 85% of users won't continue browsing a site if they see a "Not Secure" warning. So, HTTPS can really impact how long people stay on your site!

SEO Joke: Why did the SEO specialist install SSL on their dating profile? To make sure their connections were secure! 😊

---

8. Wrapping Up: Why HTTPS Matters

Switching to HTTPS isn't just a "nice-to-have"; it's a must-have for modern websites. It keeps users safe, boosts your SEO rankings, and increases your chances of making a great first impression!

Final Pro Tip 💡: If your site is still using HTTP, make the switch as soon as possible to avoid losing visitors or search engine rankings.

SEO Joke: How does a secure website greet you? With open *locks*! 😄🔒

With HTTPS and SSL in place, your website will be better equipped to handle visitor traffic securely and stand out in search results.

Module 6: SEO Analytics and Monitoring

Lesson 1: Setting Up Google Analytics and Google Search Console

Introduction to Key SEO Tools: Google Analytics and Google Search Console

Imagine if you could have a magic mirror that shows you exactly how people are finding your website, what they're doing there, and if they're enjoying the experience.

Well, Google Analytics (GA) and Google Search Console (GSC) are like that magic mirror! These two tools help you understand and improve your website's performance.

GA is like the heartbeat monitor for your website, letting you track how many visitors come to your site, how long they stay, and what pages they visit the most.
GSC is like your communication line to Google, telling you how Google sees your site, if there are any issues, and how to fix them to make sure more people find you in search results.

Why These Tools Matter

- **Understand Visitor Behavior:** See what people are interested in on your site.
- **Track Success:** Know if your site is doing well and where it needs improvement.
- **Solve Issues:** If Google can't read part of your site, GSC lets you know so you can fix it!

    SEO Joke 😊: Why did the website bring a ladder to Google Analytics? Because it wanted to "climb" the search rankings!

Setting Up Google Analytics (GA)

Let's dive into how to set up Google Analytics, step-by-step.

Step 1: Sign Up for Google Analytics

1. Go to analytics.google.com.
2. Sign in with your Google account.
3. Click on **Start Measuring**.

Step 2: Create an Account and Property

1. **Account**: Name your account (maybe use your website's name).
2. **Property**: This is like setting up a profile specifically for your website. Name it with your website URL and select your time zone and currency.

    Pro Tip 💡: If you're managing more than one website, you can create separate properties for each site under the same account.

Step 3: Get Your Tracking ID

1. After setting up your property, Google will give you a unique **Tracking ID**.
2. You need to add this code to your website to start tracking visitor activity.

Example:
Imagine you run a website called *KidsTrekWorld*. After you set up Google Analytics, GA will give you a code like UA-123456789-1. You'll place this code on each page of your website to "track" visitors.

> **SEO Joke** 😊**:** Why did the keyword go to therapy? Because it had "identity" issues without tracking!

Step 4: Adding Tracking Code to Your Website

If you have a website builder, it might let you paste your Tracking ID directly in settings. If you have someone helping with your website, ask them to add it. It's like putting your name tag on every page, so GA knows it's yours!

Navigating Google Analytics

Once you set up Google Analytics, it's time to explore!

Key Sections in Google Analytics:

1. **Home:** Quick look at your site's stats.
2. **Real-time:** See what's happening on your site right now!
   Example: If 10 visitors are exploring *KidsTrekWorld* this moment, it shows up here.
3. **Audience:** Shows you who visits your site (like age, location).
4. **Acquisition:** How people find your site (e.g., Google, social media).
5. **Behavior:** Which pages people like and how long they stay.
6. **Conversions:** Tracks actions like purchases or newsletter sign-ups.

Pro Tip ♥: Check your "Bounce Rate" in Behavior. If it's too high, people might be leaving too quickly! Try making your pages more interesting to keep visitors around.

Setting Up Google Search Console (GSC)

Now let's talk about Google Search Console – your direct line to Google! GSC shows how Google crawls and ranks your site.

Step 1: Sign Up for Google Search Console

1. Go to search.google.com/search-console.
2. Sign in with your Google account.
3. Click on **Start Now**.

Step 2: Add Your Property

1. Click on **Add Property**.
2. Type in your website URL and choose **URL Prefix** (if your site has "https://").
3. Click **Continue**.

Step 3: Verify Your Website

Google needs to know that this website belongs to you. You can verify ownership in several ways:

- **HTML Tag**: Copy a code snippet from GSC and add it to your website.

- **Google Analytics**: If you've already set up GA, you can verify through that.

Example:
Say you own *KidsTrekWorld*. By adding the HTML tag to your site's header, you're telling Google, "Yep, this is my site, and I want to know how it performs in search."

Navigating Google Search Console

Once your site is verified, you can explore some super helpful features in GSC.

Key Sections in Google Search Console:

1. **Overview:** Quick summary of your site's performance.
2. **Performance:** Shows how often your site appears in search results and which keywords bring the most traffic. *Example:* If *KidsTrekWorld* ranks for "best kids' trekking tips," it will show up here.

3. **URL Inspection:** Enter any page's URL to see how Google views it.
4. **Coverage:** Lists pages Google can and cannot crawl. *Example:* If you accidentally blocked a page, it'll appear here.
5. **Sitemaps:** Tells Google about the structure of your site so it can find pages more easily.

Pro Tip 💡: Submit a sitemap to help Google navigate your website better. Think of it as a treasure map for search engines to find all the great content you've created!

Making the Most of GA and GSC Data

Now that you have both tools set up, here's how they work together to give you the full picture.

- **GA** tells you who's on your site, what they're doing, and how they're finding it.
- **GSC** lets you know how well your site performs in Google search and if any errors need fixing.

Common Reports You'll Want to Check

1. **Performance Report in GSC:**
   Shows the keywords people use to find your site. If "best kids' trekking trails" ranks high, focus on making more related content to capture even more traffic.
2. **Audience Report in GA:**
   Understand where your visitors are coming from. If most visitors are from the U.S., you could consider adding content or services that appeal to that audience.
3. **Bounce Rate and Time on Page (GA):**
   If you see a high bounce rate, improve the page to keep people interested. A higher "time on page" means people are enjoying what they see!

   SEO Joke 😄**:** Why did the SEO expert go to school? To improve his "site" comprehension!

Wrapping Up: How GA and GSC Make You an SEO Pro

By checking GA and GSC regularly, you'll learn:

- How people find your site.
- Which keywords work best.
- Where to improve to reach even more visitors.

> **Pro Tip** 💡: Check your reports once a
> week. Consistent monitoring helps you
> spot trends and make changes that keep
> your site improving!

Quick Recap:

- **Set Up** GA to see what visitors are doing on your site.
- **Set Up** GSC to learn how Google sees your site.
- **Check Reports** in each tool weekly to see what's working and what needs fixing.

With GA and GSC on your side, it's like having a secret map to unlock all the ways to grow your website and reach more people. Happy tracking!

And there you have it—an introduction to Google Analytics and Google Search Console in a way that's easy to follow.

Lesson 2: Measuring Key SEO Metrics

Welcome to Lesson 2 of your SEO journey! In this lesson, we'll explore some of the most important SEO metrics (numbers that tell us how well our website is doing). Just like a scoreboard helps us know who's winning a game, these metrics help us understand how well our website is performing. And don't worry – we'll keep it simple and fun!

---

1. Traffic: How Many People Visit Your Website?

Imagine your website is a store. Traffic is like the number of people who come into your store every day. The more traffic you have, the more people are interested in what you offer!

- **Types of Traffic**:

- Organic Traffic: People who find your website on search engines like Google.
- Direct Traffic: People who type your website's name right into their browser.
- Referral Traffic: People who find your site from another site's link.

Example: If 1,000 people visit your website in a month, that's a traffic score of 1,000!

Pro Tip 💡: Organic traffic is like free advertising! The better you optimize your site, the more people will find you without you having to pay.

SEO Joke 😄: Why did the website bring a traffic cone? Because it wanted to direct more traffic!

---

2. Click-Through Rate (CTR): Who's Clicking?

CTR measures the percentage of people who saw your site on search engine results and actually clicked on it. It's like being in a talent show – the more people who clap (or click), the more popular you are!

- **How to Calculate CTR**: If your website appeared in search results 100 times and 10 people clicked on it, your CTR is 10%.

Example: Let's say you wrote a blog about "How to Train a Puppy." If 1,000 people saw it on Google, but only 50 clicked, your CTR would be 5% (50 clicks out of 1,000 views).

Pro Tip 💡: Make your titles exciting and eye-catching! People are more likely to click if they're curious.

SEO Joke 😄: Why did the SEO expert go broke? Because they couldn't get any clicks!

---

3. Bounce Rate: Who Leaves Right Away?

Bounce rate is like how many people leave the party as soon as they walk in. It shows the percentage of visitors who leave your site without clicking on anything. A high bounce rate means people aren't finding what they're looking for, or your page isn't engaging.

- **Ideal Bounce Rate**: If your bounce rate is under 50%, you're doing well! That means half of the people are sticking around.

Example: If 100 people visit your page, but 60 leave right away, your bounce rate is 60%.

Pro Tip 💡: Make sure the page matches what people are searching for. If your page says "Learn to Bake Cookies," make sure there's a recipe right at the top!

SEO Joke 😆: What's a website's least favorite type of bounce? The one that makes visitors leave too soon!

---

4. Average Session Duration: How Long Do They Stay?

Average session duration is like how long people stay at your party. The longer they stay, the more they like it! This metric shows the average time people spend on your site.

- **Calculating Session Duration**: If people stay for 2 minutes on average, you've got good engagement!

Example: If 100 people visit, and they stay for a total of 200 minutes, then 200 ÷ 100 = 2 minutes is your average session duration.

Pro Tip 💡: Add interesting content like images, videos, or helpful information. The more value you provide, the longer people will stay.

SEO Joke 😄: Why did the visitor stay on the SEO site for so long? They were stuck in a web of information!

---

5. Pages Per Session: How Many Pages Do They Check Out?

Pages per session tells you how many pages a visitor checks out while they're on your site. Think of it as exploring a new store – the more items (pages) they look at, the more interested they are!

Example: If 10 visitors check out 30 pages in total, that's 30 ÷ 10 = 3 pages per session.

Pro Tip 💡: Add links within your content to lead visitors to other useful pages on your site.

SEO Joke 😄: Why do visitors love exploring SEO websites? Because every page is a new adventure!

---

6. Conversion Rate: Who Takes Action?

Conversion rate tells you the percentage of visitors who take a desired action – like signing up for a newsletter, filling out a form, or making a purchase. It's like getting a goal in soccer; the more conversions you have, the better!

- **Conversion Rate Formula**: If 10 people make a purchase out of 200 visitors, your conversion rate is 5% (10 ÷ 200).

Example: If you have a button that says "Sign Up for Puppy Tips," and 10 out of 100 visitors sign up, you have a 10% conversion rate.

Pro Tip 💡: Make your call-to-action (CTA) clear and attractive! Use words like "Join Free" or "Get Started" to make people want to click.

SEO Joke 😅: Why did the website love conversions? Because it meant they'd scored big!

---

7. Backlinks: Who Recommends You?

Backlinks are like shout-outs from other websites. If a popular site links to your site, it's like getting a thumbs-up! Backlinks can improve your site's authority, which is important for ranking higher on search engines.

Example: If your blog on "Top 10 Puppy Training Tips" gets a link from a popular pet website, that's a quality backlink.

Pro Tip 💡: Focus on getting backlinks from reputable sites. One link from a trusted site can be more valuable than many from unknown ones.

SEO Joke 😅: What did the backlink say to the website? "I've got your back… link!"

---

8. How to Interpret These Metrics for SEO Insights

Now that we know what each metric means, let's look at how to use them together.

- **If Your CTR is Low**: Try improving your titles and descriptions to make them more appealing.
- **If Your Bounce Rate is High**: Make sure your content matches what visitors are searching for. Add engaging content to keep them interested.
- **If Your Average Session Duration is Low**: Consider adding videos or making the content easier to read.

Example Analysis: Let's say your site has 1,000 visitors, but a high bounce rate (70%) and low average session duration (30 seconds). This could mean people aren't finding what they want on your page. You might want to add a clear headline, relevant images, and a catchy introduction to keep them interested.

Pro Tip 💡: Regularly check your SEO metrics and adjust your content based on what you learn. Small changes can make a big difference!

SEO Joke 😄: Why was the SEO metric always relaxed? Because it could always bounce back!

Lesson 3: Monitoring Rankings and Traffic Trends

When we talk about SEO, we're always curious about how well our website is doing, right? It's a bit like playing a video game where you want to keep leveling up! Just like checking our score in a game, SEO has tools to help us track our "score" or how well we're doing on search engines and how many people are visiting our website.

Tools for Tracking Rankings and Traffic 📈

To track how our website is ranking, we use special tools. Imagine these tools as superhero glasses that let us see how many people visit our site, how high it shows up in search results, and if our SEO moves are working! Here are some tools that even a superhero would need in their SEO kit:

1. Google Analytics

Google Analytics (GA) is like a spy for your website, showing you everything happening on it! You can see how many people visit, where they come from, and even which pages they like the most.

Example: Let's say you have a blog about toys. Google Analytics will show you if people are searching for "cool robot toys" or "best dollhouse" and if they're sticking around to read or leaving too quickly.

> **SEO Joke**: Why did the SEO expert cross the road?
> To get to the other SERP! 😄 (SERP means Search Engine Results Page, by the way!)

2. Google Search Console (GSC)

Google Search Console is like a direct chat with Google about your website. GSC shows where your website ranks in search results and if there are any problems that might make it hard for people to find your site.

Example: Imagine Google Search Console is a coach helping you fix issues so your site can be the best player on the team. It might tell you if there's a "404 error" (which means a page isn't found) or if your site isn't mobile-friendly.

> **Pro Tip** 💡: Always keep an eye on "queries" in GSC! Queries are the exact words people type in search engines to find your site. Adjust your content based on what's popular—it's like taking the fastest route in a race!

3. Ahrefs and SEMrush

Ahrefs and SEMrush are tools that let you peek at what your competitors are doing. These tools track keywords and backlinks (the links pointing to your site from other sites) to help you climb higher in search results.

Example: If your site is about "pet care tips," these tools will show which pet-related keywords are hot. You can also see where other pet sites are getting backlinks and find ways to get similar ones.

SEO Joke: Why did the SEO expert bring a ladder to work?

To climb up the rankings! 😊

Analyzing Trends to Adjust Strategy 🔍

Now that we know which tools to use, let's talk about why we're using them. The key to SEO is understanding trends, or changes in how people are searching and clicking. Monitoring trends lets you spot changes in what's popular and adjust your strategy so you don't miss out.

Identifying Traffic Trends

Imagine your website as a café. You want to know when the busiest times are, which menu items are popular, and if people like your new specials. Traffic trends do the same thing for your website, showing you when people are visiting most often and which pages are their favorites.

Example: If you notice lots of traffic on Mondays for "motivational quotes," you might post a new quote every Monday morning to keep the momentum going!

> **Pro Tip** 💡: Seasonal keywords can bring in lots of visitors. For example, "winter hiking gear" might be popular in December, so plan posts around the seasons!

Tracking Rankings Over Time

Just like keeping track of your grades, tracking your rankings shows if your website is "acing" in search results. If you see your rankings dropping, it's time to review your SEO efforts.

Example: Suppose you rank #5 for "best chocolate cake recipe," but then drop to #10. Maybe more people are searching for a "quick chocolate cake recipe," so adding a quicker recipe option could help boost your ranking again.

> **SEO Joke**: How many SEOs does it take to change a light bulb?

Just one, but they need to do it five
different ways so it ranks! 😄

Adjusting Your Strategy Based on Data 📊

After identifying trends and seeing where your
rankings stand, it's time to adjust your strategy! This is
like making changes to your game plan to score higher
points.

1. Target New Keywords

If you notice new keywords getting popular, try writing
content that targets these words. It's like cooking a
new dish if people start requesting it at your restaurant.

Example: If "healthy smoothies" is trending, you could
create a new recipe post for "quick healthy smoothies
for kids."

> **Pro Tip** 💡: Use tools like Google Trends
> to see what's popular right now. Adjust
> your content for these trends, and you'll
> stay fresh in search results!

2. Update Old Content

SEO is always changing, so even your best articles need a little refresh to stay relevant. Updating old content helps keep visitors interested and boosts your rankings.

Example: If you wrote a guide on "fitness tips" three years ago, add new tips or update outdated info. This makes your content current and can help bring it back to the top of search results!

3. Keep an Eye on Competitors

Remember our tools Ahrefs and SEMrush? Keep tabs on competitors to see what's working for them, and use it to improve your site.

Example: If you notice a competitor is getting lots of visitors from a post about "eco-friendly toys," you could create similar content and add unique tips or ideas to stand out.

> **SEO Joke**: What do SEOs call people who don't follow the rules?
> Rank rebels! 😜

Wrapping Up

Monitoring rankings and traffic trends is like checking your report card in SEO. By using tools like Google Analytics, Google Search Console, Ahrefs, and SEMrush, you get valuable insights to keep your website healthy and popular. Remember to watch for seasonal trends, update your old content, and always keep an eye on competitors to stay one step ahead.

With these strategies, you're ready to make smart adjustments and grow your website's audience. Just think of SEO as a friendly game where every improvement is a win!

> **Final Pro Tip** 💡: SEO is like a marathon, not a sprint! Checking your site's performance regularly helps you spot small changes before they become big problems, and every little win adds up over time!

Lesson 4: Understanding and Using SEO Reports

In this lesson, we'll dive into SEO reports! We'll cover why SEO reports are important, how to create effective ones, and how to make them easy to understand for others who might not know all about SEO.

1. What's an SEO Report and Why Do We Need It?

An SEO report is like a report card that shows how well a website is doing in search engines like Google. Just like a school report card shows grades in different subjects, an SEO report shows grades on things like website traffic, rankings, and user engagement.

Example: Think of an SEO report as a scoreboard for your website, showing how many people visited, how high it ranks for certain keywords, and whether visitors liked what they found.

SEO Joke 😄: Why did the SEO report get sent to detention? Because it was ranking too low!

Pro Tip 💡: Make reports easy to read with clear sections and charts, so even people who don't understand SEO can follow along!

---

2. Building Effective SEO Reports

Creating an effective SEO report means focusing on what's most important. It should help people see the progress, what's working, and where improvements are needed.

A. Key Sections of an SEO Report

Each SEO report should have:

- **Traffic Analysis**: How many visitors the site got and where they came from.
- **Keyword Rankings**: How the site is ranking for target keywords.
- **Backlink Profile**: A summary of links from other sites pointing to your site.
- **Conversion Data**: How many visitors took actions, like signing up or purchasing something.

Example: For a dentist's website, the SEO report might show:

- **Traffic**: 5,000 visitors this month.
- **Keywords**: Ranking #1 for "local dentist near me."
- **Backlinks**: 10 new links from health blogs.
- **Conversions**: 50 new patient sign-ups.

SEO Joke 😂: How does SEO wish each other luck? "May the rankings be ever in your favor!"

Pro Tip 💡: Use graphs and charts for each section. Numbers are easier to understand when they're colorful and visual.

B. Comparing Month-to-Month Data

People like to see progress! Comparing data from one month to the next shows if the website is improving.

Example: In June, your traffic was 3,000 visitors, but in July, it jumped to 4,500 visitors. This month-to-month comparison makes it easy to see growth.

Pro Tip 💡: Always compare data from the previous month and the same month last year. This shows both short-term and long-term growth.

---

3. How to Present SEO Reports to Stakeholders

Stakeholders are people like business owners, managers, or clients who want to know how their website is doing. They might not understand SEO terms, so it's essential to keep the language simple.

A. Using Simple Language

Instead of saying "Bounce rate has decreased," say, "Fewer visitors are leaving right away when they visit the website."

Example: Instead of saying, "Our organic traffic increased by 30% this quarter," try, "More people are finding us on Google!"

SEO Joke 😄: What's an SEO's favorite band? Linkin Park!

B. Focusing on Goals

Find out what's important to the stakeholders. Are they more interested in traffic numbers, customer sign-ups, or sales? Highlight these in the report.

Example: If a client cares most about getting more customers, focus on how many people signed up or contacted the business.

Pro Tip 💡**:** Start the report with a "summary section" that highlights the main points—traffic, rankings, and conversions. That way, even busy stakeholders can quickly see the big picture.

---

4. Using Data to Tell a Story

Data doesn't have to be boring! Telling a story with data helps make the report more exciting and meaningful.

A. Adding Context to Numbers

Numbers make more sense with a bit of explanation.

Example: Instead of just saying, "We had 1,000 visitors," add, "This is a 20% increase from last month!" It shows that the website is improving and gives the numbers context.

SEO Joke 😊**:** Why did the SEO bring a ladder to the office? To help the website climb the rankings!

B. Explaining Changes and Trends

If traffic goes up or down, explain why it happened. Did you run a new campaign? Was there a seasonal trend? Adding this information helps make the report more valuable.

Example: Let's say there was a drop in traffic in December. You could explain that many people were on holiday, so website visits naturally slowed down.

Pro Tip 💡**:** When a trend is unusual, research the reason behind it. Maybe there's a holiday effect, a new Google update, or another reason for the change.

---

5. Tools for Creating SEO Reports

There are several tools to make SEO reports look professional, and they gather data automatically to save time.

A. Google Analytics

Google Analytics shows data on how visitors use the website. It can tell you how many people visited, what pages they looked at, and how long they stayed.

B. Google Search Console

Google Search Console shows data on how the website is performing in Google's search results. It tells you what keywords people are using to find your site and if there are any technical issues.

Example: Using Google Analytics, you can see that most people are visiting the "About" page. Using Google Search Console, you can see that the website is ranking well for "best SEO agency."

SEO Joke 😄**:** What does an SEO report need after a long day? A nap-time on the homepage!

Pro Tip 💡: Start with simple tools like Google Analytics before trying more advanced tools. It's free and has all the essentials.

---

6. Highlighting Wins and Addressing Areas for Improvement

It's essential to celebrate progress and to also address areas where improvements are needed. A balanced report is the best way to keep stakeholders happy and informed.

A. Showing Wins

When traffic or conversions increase, highlight these achievements. This helps build trust and shows the SEO strategy is working.

Example: "Traffic increased by 25% this month, and we gained 100 new sign-ups!"

B. Addressing Improvements Needed

Don't be afraid to point out areas that need work. It shows honesty and gives a clear path forward.

Example: "Our bounce rate is higher than we'd like. Next month, we'll work on making the pages more engaging."

SEO Joke 😂**:** Why did the SEO report cross the road? To get more organic traffic on the other side!

Pro Tip 💡**:** End the report with a "Next Steps" section. This helps stakeholders understand what will be done in the future.

---

7. Conclusion: Making SEO Reports Fun and Understandable

SEO reports don't have to be complicated! Keep them simple, use easy language, and focus on what's important to the client. By adding a bit of humor and context, you can make SEO reports enjoyable and effective.

Final Pro Tip 💡**:** Make the report as visual as possible. Use icons, colors, and charts to make it fun to read. People will appreciate the effort and find the information easier to remember!

SEO Joke 😄**:** How do SEO experts keep cool? They know how to chill… by ranking high with "ice-cold keywords."

Module 7: SEO Best Practices and Updates

Lesson 1: Staying Updated with SEO Changes and Google Algorithm Updates

Why Google Updates Matter for SEO

Imagine Google is a huge library, and its job is to organize and rank websites so that when you search for something, it can give you the best answer right away.

To do this, Google has rules, or "algorithms," that tell it which websites are most helpful. But here's the thing: Google loves updating these rules to make sure we all get the best, freshest answers.

When these rules change, it can impact how websites show up in search results, and this is what we call an "algorithm update."

> **Example**: Think of a school test where the rules keep changing. One week, the teacher says, "You need to show all your work!" The next week, it's "Only the final answer matters!" Websites have to keep up with these changes to stay at the top of Google's "search test."

Big Google Updates that Changed SEO

Here are some of Google's most famous updates and how they changed the SEO game.

1. **Panda Update** (2011): This one was a big deal! It made sure that websites with great, high-quality content were rewarded, and sites with poor content got pushed down in search

results.

Example: Imagine two bakers. One bakes delicious fresh bread, and the other bakes bread that tastes like cardboard. Google wanted the tasty baker to be at the top!

2. **Penguin Update** (2012): This update went after sites with "bad" links, like spammy or bought links, pushing them down in rankings.
   Example: If you're in a popularity contest but you're only friends with robots who don't really know you, it's not going to help you win! Google wanted to reward real friendships (good links) over fake ones (spammy links).

3. **Mobile-Friendly Update** (2015): Google noticed that lots of people were searching on their phones, so it rewarded websites that looked and worked great on mobile devices.
   Example: Think about a website that fits perfectly on a tiny phone screen versus one

that's so big you have to keep zooming in and out. Which one would you rather use?

4. **RankBrain Update** (2015): This one used artificial intelligence (AI) to better understand what people were searching for, helping Google connect searchers with the most helpful answers.
   Example: If you type "movie with a big green guy and a donkey," Google knows you're probably looking for *Shrek*! Pretty smart, right?

The Impact of Google Updates on Websites

Each update changes how websites rank. Some websites might find themselves on the top of the search page, while others drop lower. When that happens, people who own websites need to adjust their SEO strategies to keep up with Google's changes. The goal is to stay relevant and continue attracting visitors.

SEO Joke ☺: Why did the website go to therapy? Because it couldn't handle all the Google algorithm updates!

Resources for Staying Current with SEO Trends

Keeping up with Google's updates and the latest SEO trends can be a full-time job! But thankfully, there are many easy ways to stay in the loop. Here are some resources you can use:

1. **Google's Official Blog**: Google shares news and announcements about major updates on their official blog. Whenever there's a big change, you'll likely hear it from them first! **Example**: Imagine Google's blog is like the morning news—it's the best place to get information straight from the source.

2. **SEO Blogs** (Moz, Search Engine Journal, Ahrefs Blog): Many websites specialize in sharing SEO news and trends. Moz, Search Engine Journal, and Ahrefs are known for

breaking down complex topics into simple terms.

Example: These blogs are like friendly neighborhood teachers who help everyone understand what's new and what to do about it.

3. **Google Search Console**: This tool not only shows how your website is performing but also lets you know if there's something wrong that Google thinks you should fix.
   Example: Google Search Console is like a coach who watches your website "play" and gives advice on how to score more points (traffic).
4. **Social Media and SEO Experts**: Following SEO experts on Twitter, LinkedIn, or YouTube can be a quick and easy way to stay updated. Many experts post about recent changes and how they're adapting.
   Example: Think of SEO experts like the smart kids in class—they've studied every rule, and they're ready to share notes!

5. **SEO Tools** (Ahrefs, SEMrush): These tools provide detailed information about how updates impact your website and how you can adapt. **Example**: SEO tools are like a magnifying glass, showing you the smallest details about your website's performance so you can make improvements.

   Pro Tip 💡: Follow Google's John Mueller on Twitter or check out the Google Search Central YouTube channel for tips directly from Google insiders!

Staying Ahead: How to Adapt Your SEO Strategy

When Google rolls out a new update, it's essential to keep your strategy flexible. Here's a quick action plan you can follow to adapt quickly:

1. **Monitor Your Website's Performance**: After an update, keep an eye on your website's traffic and rankings. Sudden drops might mean it's time to adjust your SEO.

2. **Evaluate Your Content**: Google loves fresh, high-quality content. If you notice your pages losing traffic, consider adding updated info, new visuals, or helpful links.

3. **Optimize for User Experience (UX)**: Make sure your website is easy to use, loads fast, and looks good on mobile devices.

4. **Focus on Quality Links**: Build links from reputable sources and avoid any that feel spammy. The Penguin update taught us that Google doesn't like "fake friends."

5. **Keep Learning**: SEO is an ongoing process. Read articles, watch videos, and try new strategies to stay ahead.
   Example: Think of your website like a plant; it needs constant watering (updates) and sunlight (SEO adjustments) to keep growing strong!

SEO Joke 😄: Why did the website break up with its link-building strategy? Because it found too many "toxic" links!

Fun Facts and Data on Google Algorithm Updates

- **Did you know?** Google changes its algorithm about **500 to 600 times each year**! Some updates are tiny, but a few are major changes that affect millions of websites.
- **A single Google update** can impact up to **30% of search results**! This means that if a big update rolls out, many websites might notice big changes in their traffic and rankings.

Pro Tip 💡: Don't panic if a Google update affects your site's ranking! Instead, focus on understanding what changed and adjust your SEO strategy. Remember, slow and steady wins the SEO race.

Wrapping Up

Google's updates are like "rules of the road" for the web. They guide us toward creating helpful, trustworthy websites that users love. By staying updated, you'll be prepared for any twists and turns that come your way!

> **SEO Joke** 😄: Why did the SEO expert bring a ladder to work? Because they wanted to "climb" up the rankings!

In the fast-changing world of SEO, staying informed is key. The more you know, the better you'll be at creating a website that shines—no matter how many updates Google throws your way!

Lesson 2: Common SEO Mistakes and How to Avoid Them

Introduction: Oops! Don't Fall for These SEO Traps

Hey there, young SEO whiz! 👋 Have you ever tried to win a game but made a few mistakes that cost you points? SEO is kind of like that.

Making small mistakes can hurt a website's chance to rank high on search engines. But don't worry! Today, we'll learn about some common SEO mistakes and how to avoid them. Ready? Let's get started!

---

1. Not Using the Right Keywords

What's the Mistake?

Imagine you're trying to catch fish in the sea 🌊. If you use the wrong bait, the fish won't come. In SEO, keywords are like bait, but if they're not the right ones, people might not find your website!

How to Avoid It

To find the right keywords, think about what people are searching for. For example, if you're talking about pizza 🍕, you'll want keywords like "best pizza recipes" or "easy homemade pizza."

- **Example**: If you're writing about toys, using "fun toys for kids" is better than just "toys."
- **Data Tip**: Studies show that using relevant keywords can improve search rankings by up to 70%!

SEO Joke 😄

Why did the SEO expert go broke? Because they kept focusing on keywords that no one searched for!

Pro Tip 💡

Use keyword tools like **Google Keyword Planner** to find popular keywords. It's like finding the most popular bait for your fish!

---

2. Ignoring Mobile Users

What's the Mistake?

Think about how many times you've searched for something on a phone 📱. If a website doesn't work well on mobile, it's like trying to play a game that doesn't fit on the screen!

How to Avoid It

Make sure your website looks great and is easy to use on mobile. Google loves mobile-friendly sites!

- **Example**: If your website has big buttons and is easy to scroll on a phone, it's mobile-friendly.
- **Data Tip**: Over **60% of internet users** browse on mobile, so making your site mobile-friendly is super important.

SEO Joke 😄

Why was the website always last in line? It couldn't get mobile-friendly fast enough!

Pro Tip 💡

Use Google's **Mobile-Friendly Test** tool to check if your website is ready for mobile users!

---

3. Forgetting Meta Tags (Title Tags and Meta Descriptions)

What's the Mistake?

Meta tags are like the book covers of your website 📖. If they don't look good, people won't click on them. Missing or boring meta tags make your site look unappealing in search results.

How to Avoid It

Write catchy, clear, and descriptive meta tags so people know exactly what your page is about.

- **Example**: If your page is about chocolate cake recipes, a good title tag would be "Delicious Chocolate Cake Recipes | Easy and Quick!"
- **Data Tip**: Sites with strong meta tags can see up to a **40% increase in click-through rate**.

SEO Joke 😄

Why did the webpage get in trouble? It didn't have a title, so no one knew what it was about!

Pro Tip 💡

Keep your title tags under **60 characters** and meta descriptions under **160 characters** for the best results.

---

4. Overstuffing Keywords

What's the Mistake?

Imagine if I kept saying "cake" over and over while talking about a cake recipe. "Cake cake cake..." You'd get annoyed, right? In SEO, overstuffing keywords makes a page look spammy.

How to Avoid It

Use keywords naturally. Just a few mentions are enough for search engines to understand the topic.

- **Example**: Instead of saying, "Cake recipe for cake lovers who love cake," try, "This recipe is perfect for cake lovers."
- **Data Tip**: Too many keywords can lower rankings because search engines think you're trying to cheat.

SEO Joke 😊

Why did the keyword cross the road? Because it was stuffed one too many times!

Pro Tip 💡

Stick to a keyword density of around **1-2%**—that's just 1-2 keywords for every 100 words.

---

5. Skipping Alt Text on Images

What's the Mistake?

Images without alt text are invisible to search engines □□♀□. Alt text helps search engines know what an image is about, which helps people find your website.

How to Avoid It

Always add a short description to your images using alt text.

- **Example**: If you have a picture of a puppy 🐶, your alt text could be "Cute golden retriever puppy playing."
- **Data Tip**: Sites with image alt text are more likely to appear in **Google Image searches**!

SEO Joke 😄

Why did the picture get ignored? It didn't have an alt text to introduce itself!

Pro Tip 💡

Keep your alt text short but descriptive. Aim for **under 125 characters**.

---

6. Ignoring Page Load Speed

What's the Mistake?

Imagine waiting forever for a game to load. Frustrating, right? Slow pages make users leave quickly, and Google doesn't like that.

How to Avoid It

Optimize images and use faster hosting to help your page load faster.

- **Example**: Compress large image files so they don't take forever to load.
- **Data Tip**: **47% of users** expect a website to load in **2 seconds or less**!

SEO Joke 😂

Why did the web page take so long to make friends? It was too slow to load!

Pro Tip 💡

Use tools like **Google PageSpeed Insights** to test your site's speed and get suggestions on how to make it faster.

---

7. Neglecting Quality Content

What's the Mistake?

If you write content just to fill the page and it's not helpful, people won't stay. Good content keeps readers interested and makes them want to come back.

How to Avoid It

Write useful, interesting, and unique content that answers people's questions.

- **Example**: Instead of just listing "best cakes," write about "how to bake the best cakes step-by-step."
- **Data Tip**: High-quality content can improve your chances of ranking by **up to 90%**!

SEO Joke 😄

Why did the content fail the test? It didn't make any sense!

Pro Tip 💡

Use bullet points, images, and headings to make your content easy to read.

8. Not Tracking SEO Results

What's the Mistake?

If you don't track your SEO, you won't know what's working. It's like playing a game without keeping score!

How to Avoid It

Use tools like **Google Analytics** and **Google Search Console** to see which pages are popular and how people are finding them.

- **Example**: If your page on "chocolate cake recipes" is getting lots of views, keep creating similar content.
- **Data Tip**: Websites that use data tracking improve by **20% faster**.

SEO Joke 😂

Why did the SEO expert feel lost? Because they weren't tracking their results!

Pro Tip 💡

Check your SEO stats at least once a month to stay on top of your game!

Wrapping Up: SEO Success Is Just a Step Away!

Remember, even the best SEO experts make mistakes. The trick is to learn from them and avoid them in the future. Now you know the most common SEO mistakes and how to steer clear of them. With these tips and a bit of practice, you'll be an SEO superstar in no time! ✳

Lesson 3: White-Hat, Black-Hat, and Gray-Hat SEO Techniques

Welcome to Lesson 3! Today, we're diving into the world of SEO techniques: white-hat, black-hat, and gray-hat. Imagine these techniques like three different teams playing a game. Some players follow the rules, some break them, and others are somewhere in between.

Let's explore these teams, understand what each one does, and why we should always stick to playing fair!

Section 1: White-Hat SEO – The Good Guys

What is White-Hat SEO?

White-hat SEO is like the superhero team in the SEO world! They play by the rules set by search engines (like Google), follow guidelines, and focus on creating valuable content that helps people. White-hat SEO is all about honesty and giving users the best experience possible.

Key Techniques of White-Hat SEO

1. **Creating High-Quality Content**:
   - White-hat SEO is all about creating content that people actually want to read. It's like making the best comic

book – everyone loves it, and they want more!
- Example: If you're writing a blog about "The Best Toys for 8-Year-Olds," you'd research the best toys, list why they're fun, and maybe even add some pictures!

2. **Using Relevant Keywords**:
   - White-hat SEO uses keywords that match what people are searching for.
   - Example: Instead of stuffing words like "toy, toy, toy," you'd naturally add phrases like "top toys for kids" or "fun games for children."

3. **Optimizing for Mobile**:
   - Making sure your website looks good on phones and tablets (not just computers) is part of white-hat SEO.
   - Fun Fact: Did you know that over **50% of searches** come from mobile devices? That's a lot of tiny screens!

SEO Joke Time 😄

Why did the SEO expert bring a ladder to work?
Because they wanted to climb the *ranking* ladder!

Pro Tip 💡

Always put yourself in your reader's shoes! Ask, "Would I enjoy reading this?" That's how you know your content is white-hat approved.

Section 2: Black-Hat SEO – The Rule Breakers

What is Black-Hat SEO?

Black-hat SEO is like the troublemakers in the SEO world. They try to cheat the system by using tricks to get quick results. They ignore the rules set by search engines and focus on getting to the top by any means – even if it means giving users a bad experience. But watch out: search engines have strict rules and can punish websites that use black-hat techniques!

Key Techniques of Black-Hat SEO

1. **Keyword Stuffing:**

- This means cramming a page with the same keyword over and over again, even if it doesn't make sense.
- Example: Imagine a page that repeats "funny cat videos" 50 times! It doesn't sound good, right?

2. **Hidden Text**:
   - This involves hiding keywords in the background, so only search engines see it.
   - Example: A website might have white text on a white background filled with keywords like "best shoes," but visitors won't even see it!

3. **Buying Links**:
   - Some people try to cheat by buying links from other sites to make their site look more popular.
   - Example: A new site about "science projects" might buy links from random blogs just to trick search engines into thinking it's more popular.

SEO Joke Time 😄

Why did Google go to therapy?
Because it couldn't *cope* with all the spammy links!

Pro Tip 💡

Stay away from black-hat tricks! They might work for a little while, but search engines like Google will catch on and could ban your site from search results.

Section 3: Gray-Hat SEO – The In-Betweeners

What is Gray-Hat SEO?

Gray-hat SEO is a bit like mixing white-hat and black-hat techniques. It's not fully breaking the rules, but it's bending them. Gray-hat SEO is tricky – it's like walking a tightrope: one small mistake, and you could fall on the black-hat side!

Key Techniques of Gray-Hat SEO

1. **Clickbait Titles:**

- This is when websites use super catchy titles to get people to click, even if the content isn't that exciting.
- Example: "This Trick Will Make You a Millionaire Overnight!" (But it's really just a regular savings article.)

2. **Spinning Content**:
   - Taking an existing article, changing a few words, and calling it "new" is a gray-hat trick.
   - Example: Instead of writing a fresh post about "Top 10 Homework Tips," someone might copy an old article, replace a few words, and repost it.

3. **Building Link Farms**:
   - This means creating a bunch of websites just to link them all to your main website.
   - Example: Making 10 different fake websites about "home cleaning tips" that all link back to one main cleaning business.

SEO Joke Time 😄

What did the gray-hat SEO say to the black-hat SEO? "Careful, you're one *clickbait* away from getting caught!"

Pro Tip 💡

When in doubt, stick to white-hat SEO. If a technique feels a little sneaky, it probably is!

Section 4: Why White-Hat is the Best Choice!

Using white-hat techniques is the safest and smartest way to do SEO. It might take more time, but the results last longer, and you won't have to worry about penalties from search engines. White-hat SEO helps build trust with your audience and makes sure your website stays in the good graces of search engines like Google.

- **Example**: A website using white-hat SEO that consistently shares high-quality articles about "nature facts" will slowly grow a strong, loyal audience. They'll get more visitors and stay at

the top of search results because people trust
them!

SEO Joke Time 😆

Why did the website get an award?
Because it was *search engine friendly* and always
played by the rules!

Pro Tip 💡

Think of SEO like building a friendship. You have to
build trust and offer real value over time, just like white-
hat SEO!

Summary

Here's a quick recap of the different SEO teams:

- **White-Hat SEO**: The good guys who follow the
  rules and focus on great content.
- **Black-Hat SEO**: The rule-breakers who try to
  cheat their way to the top but often get
  penalized.

- **Gray-Hat SEO**: The in-betweeners who bend the rules but risk getting caught.

Fun Fact

Did you know? Over **80% of top-ranking sites** use white-hat SEO techniques because search engines love valuable, honest content!

Final SEO Joke 😄

Why don't black-hat SEOs ever get a medal? Because they *cheat* themselves out of the race!

And remember: in SEO, honesty is the best policy. White-hat techniques not only help you rank but also make your website a place people want to visit again and again.

Lesson 4: Building a Long-Term SEO Strategy

What Is a Long-Term SEO Strategy?

Imagine you're building a treehouse. You need a plan to make sure it's sturdy, can last through the seasons, and you won't fall off! SEO is just like that. Instead of a treehouse, you're building a strong website that people will visit over and over again. A **long-term SEO strategy** is like a blueprint for making sure your website grows strong and stays useful for a long time.

Here, we'll look at the main ingredients (key elements) for a solid SEO strategy that lasts, how to mix in some quick wins, and balance these with big goals down the road.

Key Elements of a Sustainable SEO Strategy 🎯

Just like a tree needs sunlight, water, and good soil, your website needs certain key elements to grow. Let's break down the main ones:

1. Quality Content 🌸

Why It's Important: Imagine you're opening a book and it's just empty pages… boring, right? For SEO, quality content is like filling those pages with interesting stories that people want to read and Google wants to show! Google ranks websites higher when they have content people enjoy.

Example: Let's say you have a website about healthy snacks. Posting articles like "Top 10 Tasty Fruits" or "Healthy Snack Ideas for Kids" will keep people coming back.

Data Fact: 90% of users click on websites that answer their questions clearly and are interesting.

SEO Joke: Why did the webpage break up with the keyword? Because it didn't *click*! 😊

Pro Tip 💡: Write for your readers first, then add keywords. Imagine chatting with a friend – make it that friendly!

---

2. Keyword Research and Targeting 🔍

Why It's Important: Think of keywords as the magic words that make your website easier to find. When people search for things on Google, keywords help connect them to the right content. But remember, you want a variety of keywords, not just the big, popular ones.

Example: If you're writing about "healthy snacks," you might include keywords like "snacks for kids," "healthy snack recipes," or even "snacks for energy."

Data Fact: Long-tail keywords (phrases that are longer and more specific) make up 70% of all web searches, and they're easier to rank for!

SEO Joke: What did one SEO expert say to another at the party? "Long time, no *see-oh*!" 😊

Pro Tip 💡**:** Use tools like Google Keyword Planner or Ahrefs to find popular keywords, and remember to include long-tail keywords that match what people might type in.

---

3. Link Building 🔗

Why It's Important: Links are like recommendations or "high fives" from other websites saying your content is trustworthy. Google loves this, and it can boost your ranking if your site has links from other good websites.

Example: If a popular food blog mentions your website and links to it, that's a big thumbs-up to Google that your website is useful!

Data Fact: Websites with strong backlinks rank higher – they get about 5x more visitors on average than sites without.

SEO Joke: Why did the SEO expert bring a ladder to work? To build better *links*! 😄

Pro Tip 💡**:** Ask for links from websites that have similar interests but aren't direct competitors. A good backlink is like a handshake from a respected friend.

---

4. Mobile Friendliness 📱

Why It's Important: More people use phones to search online than computers! If your website doesn't look good or work well on phones, people will leave. And when they leave, Google notices and won't rank your site as high.

Example: Make sure buttons on your website are big enough to tap on a phone, and that the text isn't too tiny.

Data Fact: 58% of all web searches happen on mobile devices. That's a lot of thumbs looking for info!

SEO Joke: Why did the webpage fail mobile testing? Because it *couldn't handle the touch*! 😊

Pro Tip 💡: Use Google's Mobile-Friendly Test tool to see if your site works well on phones and tablets.

---

5. Page Speed ☐

Why It's Important: No one likes waiting, especially for a webpage to load. If a page takes too long, people leave. A fast site keeps people happy and helps with Google rankings.

Example: Compress images and use fewer big files on your page. Think of it like packing light for a trip!

Data Fact: Websites that load within 3 seconds keep visitors twice as long as slower sites.

SEO Joke: Why was the website so fast? Because it didn't *drag-on*! 😆

Pro Tip 💡: Test your site speed using tools like Google PageSpeed Insights. Aim for loading times under 3 seconds!

Balancing Short-Term Wins with Long-Term Goals ⚖️□

Short-Term Wins: The Quick Gains 🪁

Some SEO moves can help you see results faster. These don't build a long-lasting "tree," but they're like planting flowers that grow quickly.

Example: Optimizing title tags and descriptions can boost click-through rates quickly. Updating your website's content with fresh info is another way to get short-term results.

Data Fact: Refreshing older content can increase traffic by up to 100% in just a few weeks.

SEO Joke: Why do SEOs love small updates? Because they're *meta-bolic boosters*! 😄

Pro Tip 💡: Set small goals like updating one piece of content each week. Celebrate those wins to stay motivated!

Long-Term Goals: Growing the Tree 🌳

While short-term moves help boost your site temporarily, the long-term strategies keep your site thriving. These include:

- Building strong content around core topics
- Earning high-quality backlinks
- Keeping your website mobile-friendly and fast

Example: Publishing a series of articles on a key topic like "Healthy Snacks" creates a helpful library for your readers and tells Google your site is an expert on that topic.

Data Fact: Websites with long-term SEO strategies have a 67% better chance of ranking well consistently.

SEO Joke: Why do SEO experts take so long to finish a project? Because they're in it for the *long crawl*! 😊

Pro Tip 💡**:** Think of SEO like gardening. Don't just plant – water it, add good soil, and prune. Update your content and monitor backlinks over time.

Wrapping It All Up 🎁

Building a long-term SEO strategy is about creating strong roots that help your website grow, attract visitors, and stay high in search rankings. Here's a quick recap of what you'll need:

1. **Quality Content** – Keep it interesting and helpful.

2. **Keyword Research** – Use both popular and long-tail keywords.
3. **Link Building** – Get thumbs-up from other websites.
4. **Mobile Friendliness** – Make sure it works on any device.
5. **Page Speed** – Keep it fast for happy users.

Balancing these key elements with both short-term and long-term goals is the best way to create a website that people love and Google ranks high. It's like building a sturdy treehouse – do it right, and people will keep coming back to hang out!

SEO Joke to End On: What's an SEO expert's favorite type of exercise? *Linking squats!* 😊

Pro Tip 💡**:** Stick with your SEO strategy! You may not see big results right away, but with time, effort, and patience, your website will become a go-to place for people looking for answers. Happy optimizing! 🎉

Module 8: Advanced SEO Topics

Lesson 1: SEO for Local Businesses (Local SEO)

Welcome to a super cool lesson on **Local SEO**! Today, we're diving into the world of local businesses and how they can shine online. If you've ever searched for "pizza near me" or "best ice cream in town," you've already used Local SEO. 🍕🍦 Local SEO is like giving a spotlight to businesses near you so they can pop up when you're looking for something specific in your area. So, let's get started!

What is Local SEO and Why Is It Important?

Imagine if you have a small pizza shop, and people in your city want to find the best pizza nearby. You wouldn't want people to have to search all over the

339

internet, right? You'd want your shop to show up right at the top when they search for "pizza near me." This is where **Local SEO** helps! It makes sure local businesses like your pizza shop can be easily found by people nearby. 💼

Fun Fact: About **46% of all Google searches** are looking for local information. That means almost half the people using Google are looking for places around them! 🔎

Step #1: Google My Business (GMB)

Google My Business (GMB) is like your online business card, but it's way more powerful. This free tool helps you show up on Google Search and Google Maps. With GMB, when someone searches for your business, they see all the important details like your address, phone number, hours, and even reviews! It's like putting a big, shiny sign in Google's window to let people know you're open for business.

How to Set Up GMB:

1. **Go to Google My Business:** Visit https://www.google.com/business and click "Manage Now."
2. **Fill in Your Business Info:** Enter your name, address, phone number, and website.
3. **Verify Your Business:** Google may send you a postcard to confirm your address. Once verified, your business is live on Google!

Example:
Let's say Sarah has a small bakery, "Sarah's Sweet Treats." When she creates a GMB listing, people searching for "cupcakes near me" will see her shop, location, hours, and maybe even pictures of her yummy cupcakes! 🍰

> **Pro Tip** 💡
> Ask happy customers to leave good reviews on your GMB page. Reviews can make your business more trustworthy and help attract new customers!

Step #2: Optimizing for "Near Me" Searches

When people search for things like "shoe store near me" or "coffee near me," they're using something called **local search intent**. This means they want results for things close to where they are. To show up in these searches, your business needs to be optimized for "near me" keywords.

How to Optimize for "Near Me" Searches:

1. **Use Local Keywords:** Include words like your city, neighborhood, or even street in your website and GMB listing. If you're a barber in Austin, Texas, you might use phrases like "best barber in Austin" or "Austin haircut near me."
2. **Location Pages on Your Website:** If you have different locations, create a page for each one. For example, "Sarah's Sweet Treats Austin" and "Sarah's Sweet Treats Dallas."
3. **Mobile-Friendly Website:** Make sure your site looks good on phones! Over **63% of all searches** happen on mobile devices. 📱

Example:
Imagine Tim has a flower shop in Chicago called "Blooming Buds." By adding words like "flower delivery

in Chicago" to his website, people looking for flowers in his area will have a better chance of finding him.

> **SEO Joke** 😄
> Why did the SEO expert keep getting lost?
> Because they couldn't find their
> "keywords" in the map app!

Step #3: Using Local Citations

A **local citation** is any online mention of your business's name, address, and phone number (NAP). Think of citations like little hints spread across the internet, helping search engines know where you are. The more accurate and consistent these mentions are, the better Google can trust your business and show it to people nearby!

Where to Get Citations:

1. **Local Business Directories:** Websites like Yelp, Yellow Pages, and TripAdvisor are great for getting citations.

2. **Social Media Profiles:** Make sure your Facebook, Instagram, and LinkedIn pages have your correct address and phone number.
3. **Local News Websites or Blogs:** Sometimes, local blogs or news sites have lists of nearby businesses. Try to get your business mentioned there too.

Example:

Imagine Emma runs a pet store called "Paws & Claws" in Seattle. By making sure her store's name, address, and phone number are the same on Yelp, Google, and her website, she's telling Google, "Hey, I'm real and I'm in Seattle!" So when people search "pet store near me," she's more likely to show up.

> **Pro Tip** 💡
> Keep your NAP details the same everywhere. If one site has "123 Main St." and another has "123 Main Street," it could confuse search engines and make your ranking go down.

Step #4: Local Link Building

Link building for Local SEO is like getting thumbs-up from other local websites. When other websites link to yours, it's like they're vouching for you, which can help Google see your business as more trustworthy.

How to Build Local Links:

1. **Join Local Events or Sponsor Them:** If there's a community event, sponsor it! Often, they'll mention your business on their website.
2. **Collaborate with Other Local Businesses:** See if nearby businesses will link to you on their website, and you can link to them on yours.
3. **Get on Local Blogs or News Sites:** Reach out to local blogs or newspapers to see if they'll feature your business.

Example:
Anna runs a bookstore, "The Cozy Corner." By sponsoring a neighborhood book fair, the event's website links back to her business. So, when people search for "bookstores near me," Anna's shop might pop up higher in the results.

Pro Tip 💡
Try to get links from local schools,
chambers of commerce, or other trusted
community sites – Google loves these! 📚

Step #5: Tracking Local SEO Success

Once you've set up GMB, optimized for "near me"
searches, and built some local links, it's time to see if
all this work is paying off. By using tools like **Google
Analytics** and **Google My Business Insights**, you
can find out how many people are seeing your listing,
clicking on your website, or calling you.

Metrics to Track:

- **Views on Google My Business**: How many
  people saw your business on Google.
- **Website Clicks**: How many people clicked
  through to your website.
- **Phone Calls**: If you get more calls, it could
  mean more customers!

Example:
Tom runs a bike repair shop. After setting up Local SEO, he checks his GMB and sees a huge increase in "Bike repair near me" searches that led to calls. That means more people are finding his business thanks to Local SEO!

> **SEO Joke** 😃
> Why did the baker do SEO?
> So their business could "rise" to the top of search results!

Quick Summary

- **Local SEO** is important for helping local businesses stand out online.
- **Google My Business** is essential. It's like your digital storefront on Google!
- **Optimizing for "near me" searches** makes sure your business shows up when people nearby are looking for what you offer.
- **Citations** help Google verify your location and trustworthiness.
- **Local Link Building** helps with rankings, too.

- **Track your progress** with tools to see how Local SEO is working.

Final Pro Tip 💡
Update your GMB page often! If you change hours, add new photos, or have special deals, keep it fresh. Google likes active listings, and so do customers! 🎉

Local SEO may seem like a lot, but with these steps, you're well on your way to attracting more customers right around the corner. Happy optimizing!

Lesson 2: International SEO Best Practices

What is International SEO?

Imagine you're playing a video game, and you want people from different countries to play it too! But people in different countries speak different languages and might even search for your game using different words. International SEO is like setting up the game so that players around the world can find it easily and understand it in their language. Just like that, international SEO helps websites reach a global audience by making sure content is visible and easy to find in multiple languages and countries.

😄 **SEO Joke:** Why did the SEO expert cross the road? To find a better rank on the other side of the globe!

---

1. SEO Strategies for Reaching a Global Audience □

If your website is targeting people from different countries or who speak different languages, you'll need to follow some international SEO strategies:

1.1 Target Specific Countries or Languages

You might want to reach people in *specific countries*, like Japan or Brazil, or *specific languages*, like French or Spanish. Deciding whether to target a country (like the UK) or a language (like English) will help Google show your website to the right people. For example, if you're selling cozy winter clothes, you might want to reach people in Canada rather than in warmer places like Hawaii.

1.2 Translating Content for Different Audiences

To reach a global audience, your content needs to be available in different languages. This isn't just about direct translation—sometimes phrases need to be adapted to fit cultural differences. Imagine if you were offering a pizza recipe: Italians might search "pizza fatta in casa," while Americans might search for "homemade pizza." The keywords change by location!

Pro Tip: Don't rely on machine translations alone; they may not capture cultural nuances. Get a local expert to review your translations!

---

2. Implementing Hreflang Tags

What is Hreflang?

The *hreflang* tag is a bit like a tiny map that helps Google know which version of your content to show based on a visitor's language or country. If you have an English version of a page and a French one, the hreflang tag tells Google which one to show to people in the UK versus France.

2.1 How to Add Hreflang Tags

You can add hreflang tags to your website's code. Here's how it looks:

html
Copy code

```
<link rel="alternate" hreflang="en"
href="https://example.com/en" />
<link rel="alternate" hreflang="fr"
href="https://example.com/fr" />
```

This code means:

- Show the English page (en) to English-speaking people.
- Show the French page (fr) to French-speaking people.

2.2 Example: Hreflang in Action

Let's say you own a website that sells comic books. You have two versions of your website, one in English and one in Japanese. By adding hreflang tags, you can make sure people in Japan see the Japanese site, while English-speaking users see the English site.

💡 **Pro Tip:** Test your hreflang tags to make sure they're working correctly. Misplaced tags can confuse search engines!

😄 **SEO Joke:** Why did the hreflang tag break up with its partner? It was tired of being "mis-placed!"

---

3. Handling Multilingual Content

When creating content in multiple languages, keeping everything organized is key. Here are some common ways to structure your multilingual website:

3.1 Using Subdomains, Subdirectories, or Country-Specific Domains

There are three main ways to set up your site for different countries or languages:

- **Subdomain:** example.fr for French content
- **Subdirectory:** example.com/fr/ for French content
- **Country-Specific Domain:** example.fr (specific to France)

3.2 Example: Organizing a Multilingual Site

Suppose you have a site about DIY crafts, and you want to reach both English and Spanish-speaking audiences. You could use:

- **Subdomain** - `es.example.com` for Spanish content
- **Subdirectory** - `example.com/es/` for Spanish content

💡 **Pro Tip:** Subdirectories are often easier to manage for SEO since all your content is on one main domain, making it easier to build authority with search engines.

---

4. Localizing Keywords for Each Country

People from different countries often search for things in slightly different ways. Localizing keywords means finding the exact words people in each country are searching for. This is essential for making your content relevant to a specific audience.

4.1 How to Find Local Keywords

There are several tools that can help with keyword research for international audiences:

- **Google Keyword Planner:** Choose specific countries to see what people are searching for in that region.
- **Ahrefs and SEMrush:** These tools let you find popular keywords in different countries and languages.

4.2 Example: Local Keyword Research

Let's say you're running an online bookstore, and you want to reach readers in both Spain and Argentina. In Spain, people might search "libros online," while in Argentina, "libros por internet" might be more common. Using local keyword research, you can adapt your content to match each search term.

💡 **Pro Tip:** Use Google Trends to check the popularity of certain terms in different countries. This helps you see if people's searches vary based on location.

---

5. Creating Culturally Relevant Content

To make your content engaging and relatable, consider cultural differences. For example, holidays, slang, and even preferences for certain types of images or colors can differ.

5.1 Examples of Cultural Relevance in Content

If you're promoting a fitness app, for instance:

- In the U.S., you might focus on New Year's resolutions for getting fit.
- In Japan, you might highlight mindfulness exercises, as there's a strong culture around well-being and balance.

💡 **Pro Tip:** Adjust visuals as well as text—some cultures prefer more formal images, while others like colorful, playful designs.

😄 **SEO Joke:** Why was the website in trouble in different countries? It had "no local appeal"!

---

6. Measuring Your International SEO Success 📈

To see if your international SEO efforts are working, you'll want to track the right metrics. Some useful tools include:

- **Google Analytics:** Check where your visitors are coming from and if certain languages or regions perform better than others.
- **Google Search Console:** Look at which countries your traffic comes from and how well pages rank globally.

6.1 Example: Using Analytics for International SEO

Imagine you're running a cooking blog. Using Google Analytics, you see that 60% of your traffic is from Spain. That's a clue that your Spanish-language content is doing well! You might then decide to create even more recipes in Spanish to keep those readers coming back.

💡 **Pro Tip:** Set up goals in Google Analytics to track actions that matter to you, like signing up for a newsletter or buying a product, in each country.

Conclusion

International SEO is about making sure that people from all over the world can find your website, read it in their language, and feel like it's meant for them.

By localizing keywords, organizing multilingual content, and using tools like hreflang tags, you're opening your website up to a truly global audience.

Remember, going global with SEO is a journey, and with every step, you're bringing your website closer to your international audience!

😄 **SEO Joke:** Why was the international SEO expert so calm? Because they had "global perspective!"

Lesson 3: Video SEO and Visual Content

Welcome to Lesson 3! Today, we're diving into how to make your videos and pictures super popular online. We'll learn about Video SEO (which helps people find your videos), the power of YouTube, and how to make your visuals stand out on search engines. Let's go!

---

1. What is Video SEO?

Video SEO is all about making videos easier to find online. When you optimize your video, you're basically giving search engines like Google a map to help them find it.

So, if you make a video about "How to Bake Cupcakes," good Video SEO helps people searching for cupcake baking tips find your video.

Example: Imagine you made a video of your dog doing funny tricks. By adding words like "funny dog tricks," "dog videos," and "cute pets" when you post, people looking for those topics can easily find your video!

SEO Joke: *Why did the video cross the road? To get more traffic, of course!* 😄

---

2. How to Optimize Videos for SEO

To make your video easier for search engines to find, try these simple steps:

A. Use Keywords in Your Title

The title of your video should match what people might search for. For example, if you have a video about "Building a Treehouse," use that exact phrase in your title.

Example: Instead of just saying "Fun Project," try "How to Build a Treehouse - Easy Steps for Kids!"

Pro Tip 💡 **:** Use keywords at the beginning of your title for the best chance of showing up in search results.

B. Write a Great Video Description

The description tells viewers (and search engines!) what your video is about. Use clear and friendly language, and include your keywords naturally.

Example: If your video is about "Drawing Cartoon Animals," your description could say, "Learn how to draw cute cartoon animals step-by-step with easy instructions! Perfect for beginners and kids who love art."

C. Add Tags

Tags are like labels that tell search engines what your video covers. Use keywords related to your video's topic.

Example: For a video on "How to Make Slime," good tags might be "DIY slime," "how to make slime at home," and "easy slime recipe."

SEO Joke: *Why did the video wear tags? So it could fit in with the cool keywords!* 😄

---

3. Using Thumbnails to Boost Video SEO

A thumbnail is the first picture people see when they find your video. It's like the "cover" of your video and should be bright, eye-catching, and show what your video is about.

Example: If your video is about "Painting with Watercolors," a great thumbnail could be a picture of a colorful painting with some brushes and paints.

Pro Tip 💡**:** Use bold text on your thumbnail so people know exactly what the video is about, even if the picture alone doesn't make it clear.

---

4. Leveraging YouTube for Video SEO

YouTube is a fantastic place to post videos because it's the second largest search engine after Google! Here's how to use it to your advantage:

A. Choose the Right Keywords for YouTube

YouTube has its own special search system. Use keywords that YouTube users often look up, and use the YouTube search bar to help.

Example: Start typing "easy cake recipes" in the YouTube search bar. You might see suggestions like "easy cake recipes without eggs" or "easy cake recipes for beginners." Use these as ideas!

B. Add Captions and Subtitles

Adding captions (the text of what's being said) is a fantastic way for YouTube to "hear" what your video is about. This helps more people (and search engines) understand it.

C. Promote Your Video

To boost views and reach more people, share your video link on other websites or social media (like Facebook, Twitter, or TikTok).

Pro Tip 💡: YouTube counts views from everywhere, so the more places you post it, the better!

SEO Joke: *What did the video say to the caption?* *"Thanks for the support, I was feeling unseen!"* 😊

5. Optimizing Visual Content for SEO

Visual content includes images, charts, infographics, and even memes! Optimizing them for SEO can help them show up in search results and attract more viewers to your site.

A. Name Your Images Correctly

Give your images filenames that match what's in the picture.

Example: Instead of "IMG_1234," name it "dog-playing-fetch.jpg" if it's a picture of a dog fetching a ball.

B. Use Alt Text

Alt text describes what's in an image for search engines and helps people with visual impairments understand the content.

Example: For a picture of a "mountain sunset," the alt text could be, "Beautiful sunset over a mountain range with orange and purple skies."

Pro Tip 💡: Keep your alt text short but specific. Describe exactly what's in the image in a few words.

SEO Joke: *Why don't search engines go on vacation? Because they'd miss all the picture-perfect views!* 😊

---

6. Understanding Video Search Engines

Did you know there are search engines specifically for videos? Besides YouTube, search engines like Google and Bing have sections where people can search only for videos. Here's how to make sure your videos show up there:

A. Choose a Good Video Platform

YouTube is great, but other platforms like Vimeo and Dailymotion also help your videos get discovered.

B. Submit a Video Sitemap

If you post videos on your own website, submitting a video sitemap (a list of all your site's videos) to Google can help it find them.

Pro Tip 💡: Most people will search YouTube or Google for videos, so focus on getting your content on those platforms first.

Example: Imagine you have a baking website with a video on "Chocolate Chip Cookies." Submitting a video sitemap tells Google, "Hey, I've got this amazing cookie video here!" Now people searching on Google might see your video.

SEO Joke: *Why did the video search engine become a chef? Because it's all about finding the right recipe!* 😄

---

7. Tips for Making Visual Content SEO-Friendly

To make images and videos that rank well, think about what people like and what search engines look for.

A. Quality Matters

High-quality images and videos attract more clicks and keep people on your page longer.

B. Add Share Buttons

Make it easy for people to share your images and videos. The more people share, the more popular your content becomes.

C. Create Engaging Visuals

Use colorful, engaging visuals that match your content and make people want to click and watch.

Example: A video on "DIY crafts for kids" might include lots of colors, happy music, and fun animations to keep kids interested.

Pro Tip 💡: Post regularly to keep people coming back for more – search engines love fresh content!

SEO Joke: *Why did the image apply for a job? Because it had the right "keywords" for success!* 😄

Wrapping Up: Video and Visual Content Are Powerful!

With these tips, your videos and images will be optimized for SEO, helping them reach a bigger audience. Remember: use good titles, add descriptions, and keep everything clear and easy to find. When you put in the effort, your visuals will start getting more attention – and more clicks!

Lesson 4: Voice Search Optimization

Growing Importance of Voice Search

Imagine you're talking to your smart speaker (like Alexa or Siri) and saying, "Hey, find the best pizza place near me!" or "What's the weather like today?" That's voice search! Instead of typing, people ask questions aloud, and voice-activated devices respond.

Why Is Voice Search So Popular?

More people are using voice search every day! Let's look at some cool numbers to see how much it's growing:

- **50% of people** use voice search daily. Imagine half of the world asking their devices questions!
- **Smart speakers** are now in almost 40% of homes in the U.S. That's a lot of people talking to their devices!
- By **2025**, experts say over **75% of all internet searches** could be voice searches.

Voice search is faster and more convenient, especially when people are on the go or have their hands full. With voice search, there's no need to type, so it's perfect when you're cooking, driving, or even brushing your teeth!

SEO Joke: Why did the smartphone get so popular with voice search? Because it always knows how to listen!

How Voice Search Changes SEO

With regular search, people usually type short phrases, like "best pizza near me." But in voice search, they ask in full sentences: "Where is the best pizza place near me?" This difference matters because it changes how we should write and optimize our content.

Voice Search vs. Traditional Search

Here's an example of how voice search is different from regular search:

- **Typing:** "Weather New York"
- **Voice Search:** "What's the weather like in New York today?"

Voice searches are more conversational and natural. They sound like you're asking a friend a question. So, to rank well in voice search results, we need to make our content sound friendly and conversational too!

Tips for Optimizing Content for Voice Queries

Let's dive into some tips to help your content stand out for voice search.

1. Answer Questions Directly

When people use voice search, they usually ask questions like "What is...?" or "How do I...?" Your job is to make sure your content answers these questions clearly and directly.

Example:

- Instead of writing, "The tallest building in the world is located in Dubai," write, "The tallest building in the world is the Burj Khalifa, located in Dubai."

Pro Tip 💡: Always include the most relevant question and answer near the top of your content. This helps search engines find your answer faster.

2. Use Conversational Language

For voice search, make your content sound like a friendly chat. Use simple sentences, everyday words, and a conversational tone.

Example:

- Instead of "SEO practices for optimal search engine performance," say, "Here are some SEO tips to help your site rank better!"

SEO Joke: Why don't SEO experts use big words? Because they want to keep the conversation going smoothly!

3. Focus on Long-Tail Keywords

Long-tail keywords are phrases people use to search in complete sentences or questions. These are great for voice search because people talk in longer sentences, not short keywords.

Example:

- Instead of targeting "best pizza," try "Where can I find the best pizza in New York City?"

Pro Tip 💡: Think about questions someone would ask aloud and use those phrases as your keywords. This will help Google recognize your content when people use voice search.

Using Data for Voice Search Success

Data can guide you in creating content for voice search by showing you what people actually ask. Tools like **Answer the Public** and **Google's People Also Ask** section can give you popular questions.

Example:

Using **Google's People Also Ask**:

- Type "SEO" in Google and look at the questions people commonly ask, like "How does SEO work?" or "What are SEO keywords?"

This will give you ideas about what questions to answer on your website!

SEO Joke: How does an SEO expert stay calm? They just *search* for inner *peace!* 😊

Structure Your Content for Voice Search

Organizing your content in a clear, easy-to-read format is essential for voice search.

4. Create FAQ Sections

Adding a "Frequently Asked Questions" (FAQ) section is an awesome way to answer common questions people may voice-search for.

Example:

- If your website is about pizza, your FAQ might include questions like "What's the best pizza topping?" or "How long does it take to make a pizza?"

These sections make it easy for search engines to find answers and boost your chances of appearing in voice search results.

Pro Tip 💡: Use clear headings like H2 or H3 tags for each question so that search engines can spot them quickly.

5. Optimize for Local Voice Searches

A huge chunk of voice searches is for local information, like "Where can I get ice cream nearby?" To rank in local voice searches, make sure to:

- List your location details clearly.
- Include keywords like "near me" or your city name in relevant parts of your content.

Example:

If you own a coffee shop, write, "Looking for the best coffee in San Francisco? Visit us for freshly brewed coffee made daily!"

SEO Joke: Why was the coffee shop's SEO so good? Because it had a *latte* of local customers!

Wrapping Up with Voice Search Optimization

Voice search is only getting bigger, so preparing your content for it now is super important. Remember:

1. **Answer questions clearly and directly.**

2. **Use a friendly, conversational tone.**
3. **Include long-tail keywords** that sound natural.
4. **Organize content with FAQs** and structured sections.
5. **Optimize for local searches** if you have a business.

Pro Tip 💡: Voice search isn't going away, so start optimizing your content today! Ask yourself, "What would someone ask aloud to find this?" and write content to answer it directly.